Forms of Modern British Fiction

Symposia in the Arts and the Humanities, No. 2

Sponsored by the College of Humanities

and the College of Fine Arts

The University of Texas at Austin

Forms of Modern British Fiction

Edited by Alan Warren Friedman

University of Texas Press, Austin & London

Library of Congress Cataloging in Publication Data
Main entry under title:

Forms of modern British fiction.

(Symposia in the arts and the humanities; no. 2)
Papers presented at a symposium sponsored by the
College of Humanities and the College of Fine Arts,
the University of Texas at Austin.
1. English fiction—20th century—Criticism and
interpretation—Addresses, essays, lectures.
I. Friedman, Alan Warren. II. Texas. University
at Austin. College of Humanities. III. Texas.
University at Austin. College of Fine Arts.
IV. Series.
PR883.F6   823'.06   75-16076
ISBN 0-292-72414-4

For David DeLaura

Contents

Acknowledgments

THANKS are due to many people who made possible both the symposium at which these essays were initially delivered and also this book. The symposium was financially and morally supported by the College of Humanities (under the auspices of Dean Stanley N. Werbow), the Humanities Research Center, and the Department of English at the University of Texas at Austin. Warren Roberts, director of the Humanities Research Center, was supportive in a number of crucial ways, as were several members of his staff: David Farmer, John Payne, and David Price. The following faculty members served as symposium moderators: Sidney Monas, chairman of the Department of Slavic Languages; and Mary Flannery, Ambrose Gordon, Joseph Kruppa, Charles Sherry, Jan Van Meter, and David Wevill, all of the Department of English. Other members of the English department assisted in other important ways; these include Jerome Bump, Bryan Dobbs, James Cox, Kathleen Mullen, and William Nance. The University Research Institute provided funds for typing the manuscript of this book.

The Once and Future Age of Modernism: An Introduction

Alan Warren Friedman

". . . on or about December, 1910, human character changed." [1] Thus intoned Virginia Woolf. She was referring specifically to the first English showing of postimpressionist French painting but had in mind revolutions occurring at that time not only in all the arts but also in the ways man thinks of his universe, his social organizations, and himself—revolutions crystallized by the names Einstein, Marx, and Freud. She was, in fact, heralding what came to be known as the "age of modernism," an age we now perceive as essentially past and whose demise may be represented by another Woolfian moment—the one in 1941 when she walked into the river Ouse and never returned. (Joyce died the same year; Conrad, Hardy, Ford, and Lawrence, in that order, had already died.) Of course, every age deems itself modern, but the one bracketed by Virginia Woolf's pronouncement and her death seems the first to be

thought both "modern" and irretrievably past, and it is
with a sense of disorientation and loss that we attempt
to take stock of consequent, and perhaps narrower,
possibilities.

In *Waiting for the End,* Leslie Fiedler writes of the
analogous situation that obtained two decades later in
this country.

> It is with a sense of terror that the practicing novelist
> in the United States confronts his situation today;
> for the Old Men are gone, the two great presences
> who made possible both homage and blasphemy,
> both imitation and resistance. It is a little like the
> death of a pair of fathers or a pair of gods. . . . At any
> rate both Faulkner and Hemingway are dead, a slow
> suicide by the bottle in one case, and a quick one by
> the gun in the other, as seems appropriate to our
> tradition; and we must come to terms with our sur-
> viving selves; yet first, of course, with them. Their
> deaths have made eminently clear what the passage
> of time had already begun to establish . . . : that these
> two writers represent to us and to the world the real
> meaning and the true success of the novel in America
> during the first half of the twentieth century.[2]

A similar assessment might well define the condition
of British fiction upon the deaths of Joyce and Woolf
in 1941, just as Virginia Woolf herself noted the
significance of Hardy's death in 1928: "When we say
that the death of Thomas Hardy leaves English fiction
without a leader, we mean that there is no other writer
whose supremacy would be generally accepted, none to
whom it seems so fitting and natural to pay homage."[3]

Though more about life than death, the essays that
follow seek to create the context for such an assessment.
They were originally delivered during a symposium,

"Forms of Modern British Fiction," held at the University of Texas at Austin in November 1972. Slightly revised and rearranged, they now structure themselves so as to shape a thesis: Hardy—the first of the modern British novelists—and Joyce and Woolf—the last— are framed by Galsworthy and his like (who were dismissed by Woolf as "materialists," anachronistic, premodern) and by self-conscious postmoderns like Durrell, Beckett, and Henry Green who may, thereby, be seen as just as anachronistic in their own way— writing after the period we call modern and yet writing as though the radical innovation we associate with the moderns remained the novel's hallmark.

Galsworthy, linked since Virginia Woolf with Bennett and Wells, is here yoked with Elizabeth Bowen and Iris Murdoch by James Gindin as writers sharing an ethical focus in their fiction. Thus, as J. Hillis Miller demonstrates in his essay on Hardy, the familiar shapes a pattern of difference. Similarly, while John Unterecker explores innovativeness in three highly idiosyncratic writers—Durrell, Beckett, and Green—the modernity defined by such writers as Hardy, Lawrence, Joyce, and Woolf, though perhaps taking numerous metaphysical leaps along the way (Mr. Gindin, in the panel discussion, speaks of "a huge wrench or S-curve"), has become something of a continuum. Iris Murdoch, for example, in her book on Sartre, emphasizes the unity of the novel:

> . . . a typical product of this post-Hegelian era . . . The novelist proper is, in his way, a sort of phenomenologist. He has always implicitly understood, what the philosopher has grasped less clearly, that human reason is not a single unitary gadget the nature of which could be discovered once for all. The novelist

has had his eye fixed on what we do, and not on what
we ought to do or must be presumed to do. . . . He
has always been, what the very latest philosophers
claim to be, a describer rather than an explainer; and
in consequence, he has often anticipated the philosophers' discoveries.[4]

If, by now, differences have become our familiars, it
may be that what actually has changed is our mode of
perceiving what we call reality.

Yet, as Mr. Miller demonstrates, differences were
Hardy's familiars, too. "Similitude," he notes, "arises
from a 'basic disparity' . . ." Thus, Tess's rape or seduction may be seen as an act of "tracing" a coarse pattern
on her flesh, which, since it "was to be," is, in a sense,
an act of repetition. Similarly, Mr. Miller—who speaks
in the panel discussion of the interpretation of narrative
fiction as having become "a kind of international and
even interdisciplinary project"—himself commits an
act of repetition in his essay on Hardy when he discusses
what he sees as the novel's three central series of actions
(sex, murder, and writing) as all involving "an act of
cutting or piercing which is paradoxical." For, as Fredric
Jameson has indicated,

The reader of [Jacques] Derrida's . . . analyses cannot
fail to be struck by the way in which they so often
seem to revert to the oldest forms of Freudian interpretation, to so-called phallic symbolism. Thus in his
study of the early "Project for a Scientific Psychology"
of Freud himself, Derrida interprets the word "Bah-
nung" ("frayage" or "piercing through," most
imperfectly translated as "facilitation" in the Standard
Edition), a term designed to underscore economic
relationships between various parts of the psyche, as
a twin image of the act of inscribing a text and of

sexual penetration: so Freud (who was well aware
of the sexual symbolism of writing "which consists
of releasing liquid from a pen onto blank paper")
is used against himself. The most completely worked
out example of such a symbolic correlation of writing and sexuality is however given in Derrida's *De
la grammatologie,* where Rousseau's description of
script as a mere "supplement" to spoken language is
shown to conceal an unconscious identification
between writing and masturbation.[5]

Hardy's *Tess* is an appropriate starting place for
Forms of Modern British Fiction, for it establishes the
context of twentieth-century literature in three crucial
ways. First, Hardy's famous phrase, "the ache of modernism," means for him the withdrawal of a sense of
god or providence in the world (Hardy said, "I've been
looking for God for fifty years and if He existed I'm
sure I would have found him."), and thus man's alien-
ation from tradition and history, and his consequent
isolation.[6] James Cowan argues that Lawrence similarly
defines the modern condition when he speaks of the
reaction against "the unholy wedlock of the industrial
revolution and Christian idealism: the one divorced
from natural cycles, the other divorced from religious
cycles, and both united in the service of the utilitarian
ethic that defined creativity as production, and progress
as the proliferation of technology." Lawrence consequently asserts "Dionysian forces to correct the imbalance on the side of Apollonian forces in decadent form,"
for he sees history as having gone out of whack, as
having lost its delicate and dynamic balance.
  This sense of discontinuity seems contradicted by
various encyclopedic and culturally oriented works of the
early twentieth century—literature, as Avrom Fleish-

man suggests in his discussion of Virginia Woolf, in which the living work of the dead is articulated as an ordered hierarchy. As Eliot warns, however, these may be no more than fragments we have shored against our ruins. Unlike their predecessors, such writers as Hardy, Woolf, Eliot, and Pound imply not the triumph of civilization but its fragility, for they know that culture is insufficient to deal with a submachine gun. In unre-produced discussion, Mr. Fleishman offers this modern view of cultural continuity:

> Civilization, we might say, is made up of all the deaths of the individuals who constitute it. It's made up of all the ineffectualities and trivialities and all the greatnesses and transcendences that individual heroes, artists, have made. Civilization is something like a mound of detritus, the *disjecta membra* of experience. The mound is something stable and enduring, but it's not exactly the way one would like to establish oneself in relation to a monument of unaging intellect, as Yeats did. It's a record of failure and misery, and it records that failure and misery in a way that can bring one's own, can resonate in tune with one's own failure, misery, and despair. It universalizes itself, let us say. It allows man to be little more than his puny experience.

Second, *Tess* is strikingly modern in its structure. Premodern novels almost invariably build toward one of those two terminal conditions, death or marriage. A worthy protagonist earns an appropriate marriage (in *Moll Flanders, Pamela, Tom Jones, Pride and Prejudice, Jane Eyre, Middlemarch*) or else some moral imbalance demands death as a means of restoring equilibrium (*Clarissa, The Man of Feeling, The Monk*). Much of the excruciating tension in *Tess* results from its intertwining of these disparate plot lines, for the two are morally, aesthetically, and emotionally contradictory, yet both endings are inevitable for Tess and neither really terminates "the heroine's stream of experience." [7]

Finally, *Tess* also anticipates the tag and technique associated with such early modern writers as Ford and Conrad, for Hardy speaks in his preface of the novel's contemplative passages being "charged with impressions. . . . Let me repeat that a novel is an impression, not an argument . . . [and a taleteller] writes down how the things of the world strike him." In her essay on Hardy, Woolf quotes him to the same effect, " 'Unadjusted impressions have their value, and the road to a true philosophy of life seems to lie in humbly recording diverse readings of its phenomena as they are forced upon us by chance and change.' " [8] And in so saying, Hardy sounds indistinguishable from his ostensibly very different later contemporary, Joyce, who, as Charles Rossman quotes him, says, "I have written *Dubliners* . . . with the conviction that he is a very bold man who dares to alter in the presentment, still more to deform, whatever he has seen and heard." Thus, we enter a fictional world at odds with inherited concepts of author, plot, character, and time, one that leads finally—as Mr. Unterecker suggests—to the wholly solipsistic, discontinuous, and indeterminate in such writers as Beckett, Burroughs, and Robbe-Grillet.

Although he does not employ the terms, tradition and solipsism are also central to Mr. Rossman's essay on Joyce. His analysis of *A Portrait of the Artist,* and of its isolate figure who must go forth to create in a world he must simultaneously create, accepts the difficult challenge that Wayne Booth implicitly hurls at twentieth-century critics when he defines what he sees as that novel's hopelessly ambiguous attitude toward its protagonist.[9] For like its analogs, the journey and the education, spiritual autobiography—a mainstay of the traditional novel from *Moll Flanders* to *The Way of All Flesh*—becomes problematical and modern in Joyce largely because of uncertainty concerning distance between author and protagonist.

Nearly contemporaneously with *Portrait,* Yeats (a major influence on Joyce and cited by Stephen in the diary section concluding *Portrait*) wrote his own spiritual autobiography. The first volume, *Reveries over Childhood and Youth,* ends with a self-analysis that seems a mirror image for Stephen's hymn to life concluding *Portrait:*

> For some months now I have lived with my own youth and childhood, not always writing indeed but thinking of it almost every day, and I am sorrowful and disturbed. It is not that I have accomplished too few of my plans, for I am not ambitious; but when I think of all the books I have read, and of the wise words I have heard spoken, and of the anxiety I have given to parents and grandparents, and of the hopes that I have had, all life weighed in the scales of my own life seems to me a preparation for something that never happens.[10]

But the two works share a common perspective. Where nineteenth-century autobiography seems impelled by a need to reify the past, that of Joyce and Yeats radically breaks with tradition by seeking to purge the past— as psychoanalysis does—so that they may go on to their greatest achievements. (Mr. Fleishman similarly speaks of Woolf's early fiction, like Eliot's "Prufrock" and Pound's "Hugh Selwyn Mauberly," as prefiguring later and greater works.) The Stephen we see is necessarily ambiguous because he is not Joyce but a surrogate for him, and Mr. Rossman, by stressing *both* his "*authentic potential* as an artist" and his bitter failure, reconciles the contradictory views of Stephen that Booth finds irreconcilable. As Mr. Rossman puts it: "The Dublin minotaur has affronted Stephen and piqued him into healthy flight. But it has crippled him, wounded him so deeply that he is incapable of genuine escape, rather than mere escapism. He is trapped in a perpetual cycle: the dream of illusory liberty followed inevitably by the humiliating puncture of the dream— for reality validates itself and cannot be denied indefinitely." One response to Booth's complaint lies in the sort of praise that Mr. Miller, in unreproduced discussion, heaps on Hardy's *Jude the Obscure* precisely because of its ambiguity. "*Jude* is a beautiful case of a novel itself presenting four or five different possible ways to account for what happens to Jude, which it seems to me very hard to have all at once. You can make a whole list of seemingly incompatible explanations. It leaves you then with a novel which is quite enigmatic, I think." But Mr. Rossman takes Booth on directly and responds in a way that does not deny the tradition of autobiography inherited by the twentieth century, but focuses on the individual talent and radical displacement that Joyce brings to it.

Mr. Unterecker similarly views Henry Green's autobiography, *Pack My Bag,* as problematical, for the past "has become an illusion seen through the soft-focus lenses of memory, 'what one thinks has gone to make one up,' a thing not of vision but of revision, a thing, finally, of pure *seeming,* 'what seems to have gone on.' " Central to what Mr. Unterecker finds modern in the writers he discusses is a mode of apprehending reality that differs markedly from that of their literary forebears. "Reality is a good deal harder to pin down now than in earlier generations—largely because we have noticed that, the closer we get to it, the harder it is to see. Perhaps, indeed, our most important twentieth century observation has been that, as the mode of apprehending reality changes, reality itself undergoes significant changes. What there is depends almost entirely on how we see."

If one of the qualities of nineteenth-century fiction is its emphasis on the consciousness of consciousness, on a narrator who depicts the consciousness of other individuals, then writers like Durrell and Beckett refine a metaphysics of consciousness, a consciousness of self-consciousness, of self-reflexiveness, a perceiving stance that defines reality as existing in neither the subjective nor the objective—those two discredited terms—but *solely* in the interchange between them. "Reality," as Mr. Unterecker puts it, "becomes the illusion of coherence," and calls to mind, perhaps with a new wrinkle, Forster's epigraph to *Howard's End:* "Only connect."

One might, finally, settle for a truism: every artist is different from his predecessors because he knows more, but of course *they* are what he knows. Yet surely this will not satisfy where modern art is concerned, for, in a sense, some modern artists have asserted their own validity by implying that their predecessors are precisely what they do *not* know. The bursting of what were felt to be inherited constrictions in both subject matter and technique was bound to be traumatic; this was especially true for fiction, which since its inception has been firmly rooted in history and forms of social life—but not any more. As the essays and the panel discussion that follow demonstrate, that comfortable, mimetic relationship between the fictive realities of art and life can no longer be assumed, for, as John Donne—a modern writer three centuries ago—foresaw, "the new philosophy calls all in doubt."

Once more, Virginia Woolf is our touchstone; Mr. Fleishman concludes his essay by seeing her "as an artist fully at one with the modern movement of experimentation and innovation, but, as is the case with the other major figures of the period, her novelty is most often a variation on a traditional theme, her discovery is characteristically an insight into truths of long standing in our culture." As always, we must think the world through, and anew; and in the essays of this symposium six disparate critics suggest six different ways of doing so. That no one of them has an inherently greater claim on our attention may well be the first and ultimate lesson they can teach us about the post-modern and yet again modern world we are called upon to create along with them.

Notes

1. Virginia Woolf, "Mr. Bennett and Mrs. Brown," in *The Captain's Death Bed and Other Essays* (New York: Harcourt, Brace, 1950), p. 96.

2. Leslie A. Fiedler, *Waiting for the End: The Crisis in American Culture and a Portrait of 20th Century American Literature* (New York: Stein and Day, 1965), p. 9.

3. Virginia Woolf, "The Novels of Thomas Hardy," in *The Second Common Reader* (New York: Harcourt, Brace, 1960), p. 222.

4. Iris Murdoch, *Sartre: Romantic Rationalist* (London: Bowes & Bowes, 1965), p. 8.

5. Fredric Jameson, *The Prison-House of Language: A Critical Account of Structuralism and Russian Formalism* (Princeton: Princeton University Press, 1972), pp. 178–179.

6. For a fuller discussion of this, see David J. DeLaura,

14 | Alan Warren Friedman

" 'The Ache of Modernism' in Hardy's Later Novels," *ELH: A Journal of English Literary History* 34, no. 3 (September 1967): 380–399.

7. For a fuller discussion of closed and open endings in general and particularly in *Tess,* see Alan Friedman, *The Turn of the Novel* (New York: Oxford University Press, 1966), pp. 15–37, 51–65.

8. Woolf, *Second Common Reader,* p. 230. Woolf comments, "Certainly it is true to say of him that, at his greatest, he gives us impressions; at his weakest, arguments."

9. See Wayne C. Booth, *The Rhetoric of Fiction* (Chicago and London: University of Chicago Press, 1961), pp. 323–336.

10. *The Autobiography of William Butler Yeats* (New York: Collier Books, 1967), p. 71.

TWO

Ethical Structures in John Galsworthy, Elizabeth Bowen, and Iris Murdoch

James Gindin

IN "Mr. Bennett and Mrs. Brown," her famous 1924 avant garde manifesto, Virginia Woolf made "the surpassingly rash prediction" that "we are trembling on the verge of one of the great ages of English literature." [1] Trumpeting the energy and imagination of her own new age, praising Eliot despite what she saw as his "obscurity" and Joyce despite "indecency," Woolf saw herself and other Georgians as extracting a centrality or essence from humanity in contrast to the dense, trivial, and materialistic treatments of experience in the work of the distinguished Edwardian triumvirate —Wells, Bennett, and Galsworthy. She used "Mrs. Brown," a drab figure in a railway carriage, as a metaphor for the subject of literature:

> There she sits in the corner of the carriage—that carriage which is travelling, not from Richmond to

Waterloo, but from one age of English literature to the next, for Mrs. Brown is eternal, Mrs. Brown is human nature, Mrs. Brown changes only on the surface, it is the novelists who get in and out—there she sits and not one of the Edwardian writers has so much as looked at her. They have looked very powerfully, searchingly, and sympathetically out of the window; at factories, at Utopias, even at the decoration and upholstery of the carriage; but never at her, never at life, never at human nature. And so they have developed a technique of novel writing which suits their purpose; they have made tools and established conventions which do their business. But those tools are not our tools, and that business is not our business. For us those conventions are ruin, those tools are death.[2]

The implications of this statement for the development of Woolf's novelistic technique, as well as that of others, are many, but they are not my subject here. Rather, I am concerned with both the subsequent literary history and the implications of the assumption that there is, in human personality, a constant core, a knowable essence, a central nature that is more true and more important than any of the peripheral or accidental trappings in which it appears. Arnold Bennett, in his *Journal,* compared the novelist's knowing other people to stripping off the layers of the onion but questioned which layer was most interesting, most valuable, most important;[3] Virginia Woolf, however, saw the onion as molded by the core and thought discussion of the exterior layers a materialistic and irrelevant distraction. She doubted her own skill, sometimes her imagination, her means of reaching the core. But she never doubted her metaphysics.

Virginia Woolf's assumption is visible in her fiction, represented variously by the lighthouse that is finally reached or by the waves that ceaselessly prevent discovery and articulation of the core or by the momentary recognition that "there it is." This assumption has also been shared by enough writers, critics, and knowledgeable readers over the past 50 years to exist as something of an article of faith in our common critical judgments. One recent intelligent critic, Calvin Bedient, whose attitude is not at all unusual, measures greatness in fiction by the author's revealed capacity to discover and transform his deepest self in terms of an ideal metaphysic. In his view, only three British novelists of the last 150 years really conform to the demanding standard, for George Eliot, Forster, and Lawrence are the "three supreme creative consciences, the three major architects of the self in English fiction." [4] Virginia Woolf, as novelist, may not quite make greatness on this stringent criterion, but, as essayist, she won her propaganda appeal in the consciousness of many of those seriously interested in literature (although to what extent she created and to what extent reflected that consciousness is an open question). Many critics and serious readers value most highly fiction that either expresses a core, a fundamental entity of human personality, or creates a world, a consistent cosmos with a discernible metaphysic. Critics praise the sense of creation, both as a technical ordering of great magnitude and difficulty and as a metaphysical vision that works through and transforms human muddle and complexity. I am thinking of novelists like Lawrence and Joyce, even of Virginia Woolf herself, artists whose versions of human experience create an imaginative world. cohere around a metaphysical or essential core, and derive their force and appeal from a concept that there is, within the fiction, no way of getting beyond. And critics tend, I think, to call that fiction "great," to distinguish it from the merely "good" fiction that reflects and comments on human experience, that is, ultimately and metaphysically, as perplexed as are most of us most of the time. "Great" fiction, critics and teachers often assume, transcends and transforms our questions; "good" fiction simply reflects them. E. M. Forster stated this usual distinction succinctly when he said that *The Old Wives' Tale* is a very good but not a great novel, because its underlying theme is simply that we grow old and die and "a great book must rest on something more than an 'of course.' " [5] And, by these standards, the Edwardians—who generally were not metaphysical, did not transform ordinary experience, and did not assume an essential core of personality—would be consigned to a second, and reduced, circle of worth. The distinction between "great" and "good" is not applicable only to a particular period of literary history, for the same kinds of judgment are frequently applied to more contemporary names. Although more arguably than Joyce and Lawrence, Beckett and Camus also transform experience, seem to innovate both technically and metaphysically, and create consciousness around a metaphysic. And they are, therefore, often thought of as illustrating a higher order of fiction than do, for example, Angus Wilson or Saul Bellow.

I think, however, that this is not always a useful way to judge fiction. I have no desire to reverse the designations of "great" and "good"; in fact, I'm rather skeptical about the value of applying those distinctions critically to our accounts of what we read. Unless we all assent to the metaphysical position involved, I wonder if distinction on what is ultimately a metaphysical basis can serve as the basis for an evaluative judgment about literature. At any rate, there is another well-established line of fiction running through at least the last fifty years, fiction that is not metaphysical and does not transform experience, a kind of fiction that seemed to Virginia Woolf external, trivial, and muddled. Closer to verisimilitude, communicative to readers through the texture of ordinary experience rather than by the shape of a vision or the coherence of a self-enclosed world, this fiction is more concerned with relationships between personalities than with an essence of human personality. Characters, perhaps ultimately unknowable or without discernible core, are seen in terms of their actions and reactions to others, given life and density by what they do, say, think, and feel, rather than by what they, in some profound sense, are or represent. And because, in the world of these novels often consigned to the second circle of value, no metaphysical coherence is implied, the authors frequently devote their attention to ethical questions, speculations, and judgments. In much the same way that some of the famous literary Victorians could substitute a concept of duty for immortality or of poetry for religion, these novelists substitute an ethical concern for the metaphysical statement about the nature of man and his universe that they cannot or will not make. The interest in actions, in relationships, makes the judgments about these actions and relationships, the ethical judgments, the evaluation of what man *does* to himself and to others in this world, central to the fiction. The ethical focus, allowing the author to deal with both public and individual problems, demonstrating interest in the variety and complexity of human relationships, does not prevent readers and critics from evaluating the fiction, from judging it on the often difficult and arguable bases of intelligence, technique, or applicability to human experience. Distinction between "good" and "bad" (as well as all the various stages and qualifications in between) can be made in strictly human terms; distinction between "good" and "great," however, requires some kind of transformation, some separation of the merely human from the more than human.

Although Edwardian fiction and fiction with an ethical focus are not synonymous, the two categories sometimes coalesce. Through the nineteenth century, ethical values drifted farther and farther away from their earlier theological or metaphysical moorings and yet remained important, even assumed the particular intensity of deliberate substitutes. In fairness to both Woolf and my own introduction, I ought to meet her on her own grounds in describing more specifically the fiction of an author whose central focus is ethical, and I have chosen Galsworthy. John Galsworthy's chronicles, which span almost fifty years of English upper-middle-class and aristocratic life, avoid the extension of humanity into either a universal, central core or a grand metaphysical meaning. Joseph Conrad wrote to Galsworthy as early as 1898 about *Jocelyn:* "In fact the force of the book is in its fidelity to the surface of life—to the surface of events—to the surface of things and ideas. Now this is not being shallow . . . the achievement is as praiseworthy as though you had plumbed the very ocean. It is not your business to invent depths—to invent depths is not art either. Most things and most natures have nothing but a surface. A fairly prosperous man in the state of modern society is without depth—but he is complicated—just in the way you show him." [6] Even if Conrad felt his praise to be more ironic than anything the statement explicitly reveals, the description is apt as far as it goes. And Galsworthy invariably organizes his surfaces around ethical questions, around how a man relates with and behaves toward others. *Jocelyn,* for example, dramatizes debates about adultery. Conrad is also, I think, right in saying that Galsworthy is not shallow, for the latter, in his fiction, frequently considered possible versions of man's deepest soul or God and explicitly rejected them. God, most often, is either a respectable convention for some of the older characters or an issue about which undergraduates speculate enthusiastically but inconclusively. The soul has no depths, and, for Galsworthy, deluding oneself that it does leads to unethical behavior, unwarranted impositions on others. The lack of a metaphysical truth makes the focus on behavior, the ethical substitute, all the more important. In *End of the Chapter,* Galsworthy's final trilogy, Dinny Charwell, the central character and positive example, insists, to her own disadvantage, on behaving "better" (more considerately toward others) because she does not believe in Providence or an afterlife, and because "decency's the decent thing." [7] This consciously ethical behavior, a kind of self-punishment, even self-laceration, from perspectives other than Galsworthy's (Thomas Hardy's, for example), characterizes many of the figures he sees as admirable. Galsworthy even suggested to his publisher that *The Man of Property* should carry a subtitle, like *National Ethics I,* that indicated it was to be the first in a series of studies on ethical questions.

The Man of Property, the first novel in *The Forsyte Saga,* establishes the conflict between property and beauty, castigates the concentration on property in nineteenth-century England that led so many to assume that they could own or buy beauty and love, the emotions of the intangible in human experience. Property is represented by the Forsytes, a large family of acquisitive parasites who buy whatever is measurable and hold it to themselves, as they hold on to life itself with merciless tenacity. Beauty is represented by Irene, the rather symbolic figure who can express herself only through music. And, in the episode that reverberates through the entire trilogy, Soames, the most complete Forsyte of his generation, rapes his wife Irene to prove his ownership. For Galsworthy, the rape, the forcing against her will, the violent insistence on possession, is crucial. Beauty can never be possessed. The artist, in contrast to the Forsyte, is the person who can appreciate beauty, who can create because he is able to understand and to avoid imposition. Yet not all artists are equally worthy in Galsworthy's terms: Bosinney, Irene's first lover, can genuinely create, but he is so outraged when he learns of Irene's rape that he loses his own balance in a chaos of rage and becomes, although treated sympathetically, as intractably the artist as do June Forsyte's truculent lame ducks. Even Edward Garnett, Galsworthy's usually sensitive publisher, misunderstood the issues in the novel when he wanted Galsworthy to have Bosinney and Irene go off together joyfully at the end of *The Man of Property.* Concern with art is never, in itself, sufficient. June's gallery and her support of various narrow fads are part of her possessiveness, her anti-Forsyte Forsytism. And the later Soames, the knowledgeable collector, treated with more compassion than he was in the first trilogy (although never, as some critics have suggested, becoming Galsworthy's spokesman), is still, in his focus on ownership, cemented in the intensity of possession, just as his emotions fix with self-sacrificing intensity on his daughter. Intensity and self-sacrifice are not part of Galsworthy's requirements for the ethical artist in the modern world.

Rather, the artist who can fully appreciate beauty is

young Jolyon, the tolerant, the amiable, the open. Son
of the leader and least typical of the Forsyte clan (the
intensity of Forsytism increases among later siblings,
and the eldest son of the eldest son has the best chance
to escape a family stereotype), young Jolyon has
responded to beauty and emotion, has kept his balance
in a series of difficult family circumstances, and has
earned, finally, the gift of beauty—Irene. He is also an
artist, though a rather muted one. He paints watercolors
that achieve a modest recognition; he tolerates the in-
tensities on either side of him; he acts strongly only in
response to an imposition from the outside, another's
attempt to use or control him. In Galsworthy's terms,
his genuine artistry is suffused with a kind of gentle-
manly moderation, a refusal to establish himself as
intense: "To take himself seriously, yet never bore
others by letting them know that he did so, seemed to
have been his ruling principle." [8] This moderate, un-
assertive kind of art, one that would only smile at
"trembling on the verge of" greatness, is, for Galsworthy, the only kind that genuinely understands
beauty, that is sufficiently open and tolerant to accept
the sensations of beauty, of emotion, in any of their
various forms. Galsworthy makes ethical demands on
his artists and is more interested in the actions of the
creator than in the artistic product, more interested in
responsiveness than in the permanence of response.
Appreciation of art and a wise passivity, a refusal to
impose, are part of the same desirable sensitivity.

Young Jolyon is, however, far from the perfect
articulation of the author's point of view. On matters
other than art, on ethical questions that surround his
role as father, he is seen as vulnerable in spite of all his
good intentions. While he is in Paris with Irene, before
they marry, his oldest son, Jolly, joins a regiment to

fight in the Boer War as a result of a juvenile competition of postures with Val Dartie. When Jolly dies in South Africa, Galsworthy does not point an accusatory finger at the father, but he does leave young Jolyon with sufficient guilt and the reader with sufficient doubt to convey some skepticism about the tolerant artist's capacity as a father. When Jon falls in love with Fleur, he suffers considerable agony and a sense of unknown pressure because his parents, young Jolyon and Irene, delay telling him for so long the background of their strong objections. Galsworthy questions their own motives, their concern for themselves behind their genuine concern for Jon, just as he opens, from numerous different points of view, all the ramifications of protection and communication between parent and child. Although young Jolyon can share with Irene the responsibility for his decision to protect Jon for too long, he alone is responsible for an irrelevant tirade against youth that he, by this time old and ill and troubled, delivers when Jon brings Fleur to tea. Clearly, for Galsworthy, no man, in himself, is a completely reliable and constantly ethical perspective. Himself the son of a father kind and understanding, though a shade too rigid, too imposing, young Jolyon is a shade too hesitant, too unwilling to impose; and, partly as a consequence, young Jon develops his genuine conceptions of honor a shade too priggishly. Fatherhood is, in Galsworthy's terms, a good deal more difficult to manage ethically than is the wise appreciation of beauty and art.

In the second trilogy, *A Modern Comedy,* the public ethical focus shifts away from the artist to the man involved in politics and society, Michael Mont. And Fleur, less a representation of beauty than Irene, rather a representation of feeling or emotion, can also not be owned or possessed. Michael is able to live with Fleur, to love her despite the sometimes unbalanced intensity of her emotions, just as he is able to express concern for society in his willingness to entertain various political solutions: socialism, a plan for emigration to the dominions, a scheme for reclaiming slum houses. None of these political solutions would benefit Michael personally, and none represents a commitment so intense that other possibilities are ruled out. Rather, in his understanding and tolerant way, his concern for social and political justice is both more open and more constant than intense devotion to a single cause would permit. The single cause, like the concentration on one woman's absolute fidelity, is itself possessive; the understanding and ethical man must retain a wider view of humanity. And Michael, working in personal and political terms, becomes, for Galsworthy, the parallel to young Jolyon's center of artistic sensitivity in the first trilogy. Unlike most important characters in Galsworthy's continuous chronicle, Michael and young Jolyon never meet. Young Jolyon dies at the end of the first trilogy, his function accomplished, and Michael appears at the beginning of the second. In contrast, Irene and Fleur, beauty and emotion, are always simply there.

Young Jolyon and Michael Mont are always historically conscious; they recognize that particular issues change, that what is ethical or appropriate in terms of one generation or society is not so in another. Realizing that he might, at a different time and under different circumstances, react in a very different way, Michael is charitable to a poor packer who steals books from the publishing firm to sell on his own. In another episode,

Michael recognizes that Fleur can win her slander suit against Marjorie Ferrar in a courtroom that enshrines principles of honor that belong to a past age, but she loses the same suit in the judgment of contemporary society on principles that Galsworthy sees as no less moral than those of the court. The frequent courtroom scenes in Galsworthy's fiction are, in fact, dramatic forums for ethical debate, not at all the revelations of unexceptionable truth so common in the kind of drama that solves mysteries. And an event like the 1926 General Strike, a vast social conflict in which right or wrong is impossible to assign to either side, leads Galsworthy to concentrate on the ethics of how various characters act in terms of the side toward which their commitment is socially predetermined. Fleur can, in part, define herself as an extraordinarily efficient canteen manager, Jon as a fireman on a train; Michael, however, who sees the issue so much more comprehensively, must just wait through the polarities of social conflict until his more far reaching solutions have a chance to operate again.

All the issues of social change, business ethics, the morality of what one man can say to another in his club or in his house are filtered through the perspectives of young Jolyon and Michael, men always conscious of being part of a certain time and place and, therefore, less unequivocally committed than are some others to the values of that time and place. Both, too, appreciate the sense of civilization, the sense of tolerance, they feel fortunate enough to share with other late-nineteenth- and early-twentieth-century Englishmen. At the end of *A Modern Comedy,* when he guesses that Fleur has been unfaithful to him and has been rejected by Jon, Michael articulates his response, his knowledge that he will accept the situation, in historical terms:

All his life he had detested the ebullient egoism of the *crime passionnel,* the wronged spouse, honour, vengeance, "all that tommy-rot and naked savagery." To be excused from being a decent man! One was never excused from that. Otherwise life was just where it was in the reindeer age, the pure tragedy of the primeval hunters, before civilization and comedy began.

Whatever had been between those two—and he felt it had been all—it was over, and she "down and out." He must stand by her and keep his mouth shut.[9]

Civilization is far from just or equitable, and, even at his widest, Galsworthy is dealing, as he indicates in his preface to *A Modern Comedy,* with only that "tenth or so of the population whose eyes are above the property line"[10] (the other nine-tenths have demonstrably fewer choices). At the same time, his characters live within a civilization, are in part defined by it, and must, if they are to survive wisely, respond within civilization's terms. Primitivism, the sweeping away of a civilization in favor of some expression of the primal self or some core of personality, is intense and destructive, likely to be a more severe imposition on others than is any civilized compromise or inequity. Within the civilization, however, terms and issues and responses constantly change. In her last appearance in *End of the Chapter,* Fleur—now a competent, stable, and understanding young matron—can say, in reference to her father's raping of Irene, the issue that propelled so much of the saga and that, indirectly, led to Fleur's existence, that "the woman made a great fuss for nothing much."[11] Galsworthy's edge of irony seems to be directed, in about equal proportions, against Fleur's impercipience and against those who might think any issue, no matter how dramatic and significant, capable of remaining visible in the same terms through changes in time.

End of the Chapter continues Galsworthy's ethical focus on political issues involving Englishmen in a changing world. Each of the three novels follows one of the Charwell children, cousins of Michael Mont, although the ethical focus is always that of Dinny, the middle child and open-minded counterpart of Michael and young Jolyon. Dinny also gains support and advice from three loving uncles, a wealthy baronet, a slum-clearing cleric, and an anthropologist—a triumvirate representing the best of sane, moderate civilization. In the first novel, Hubert, a military man, has killed a native in self-defense while on a South American expedition; in the second, the poet to whom Dinny is engaged, privately agnostic, has been forced at knife-point, while in the Middle-East, to become a Muslim convert; in the third (the weakest novel), Dinny's younger sister, separated from a brutal husband, spends a night in a car with another man. In all of these, the specific issue can be seen, from certain points of view, as trivial. But Galsworthy's point is that—in a civilized society—individual political, religious, and sexual issues ramify, must be judged and acted upon in terms of a wide social context. None of the characters is able to act solely in terms of intensely individual integrity, although all are capable of following strong feelings. At the same time, respectability, convention, acting out a consensus of opinions so freely discussed in London clubs and drawing rooms, is also not the solution. Rather, as Dinny finally sees in each separate novel, the adjustment between society's claims and individual integrity is complicated and difficult, requires working through separately in terms of each individual issue (if, for example, the ethos of colonialism is implicitly endorsed in the second novel, it is not in the first), and is vulnerable to a complexity of individual and social response. And, as always in Galsworthy, the ethical perspective is intelligent and sympathetic in the midst of all the lively and bewildering detail of twentieth-century civilization. Galsworthy never advocates the intensity of cores or metaphysical truths.

Fiction with a human and ethical focus has also been highly visible since the time of the Edwardians, despite the critical ideas engendered by a renascence of the quest for metaphysical certainties in the 1920s. In American fiction, for example, both Hemingway and Fitzgerald began with an attitude rather like an ethical assertion in the face of a metaphysical void. Hemingway extolled the courageous man who faces an ultimate nothingness with grace and dignity; Fitzgerald, in *The Great Gatsby,* was the moralist who can understand but does not finally engage in the corruptions, myths, and cruelties of the society around him. But the two novelists moved in different directions: for Hemingway, the ethical stance became a kind of metaphysical pose, assumed a certainty, an intransigence, that finally blocked any further ethical speculation or the treatment of other dimensions of humanity; Fitzgerald, on the other hand, in *Tender is the Night* and what exists of *The Last Tycoon,* widened his framework and considered more of the ethical implications of sexual, economic, political, and American experience, even though something of the capacity to judge that experience had dissipated. In his later work, the ethical focus as the central question, the central concern communicated to the reader, remains and radiates.

Another novelist whose distinguished work in the 1930s can be seen through its ethical focus is Elizabeth

Bowen. Often relegated by critics to the condescending
category of the sensitive female novelist, pushed, along
with Virginia Woolf, into the designation of the
merely perceptive, Bowen wrote novels the aim of
which was very different from Woolf's. Both *The
House in Paris* and *The Death of the Heart* show
young characters, inhibited by conventional righteous-
ness, seeking a wider understanding and a more richly
human morality from the past. Those adults who
represent society attempt to cover up the past, obliterate
history; but the new generation, sometimes aided by the
old family servant, that traditional novelistic device
for wisdom enduring through generational changes,
uses its sensitivity to confront and live with the implications of the past. Like Galsworthy, then, Elizabeth
Bowen deals with history and generations, with the
changes in and transmissions of ethical values from
one generation to another. In addition, for both novelists, morality involves relationships, the quality of
interchange between one person and another, and cannot be developed in isolation. But instead of Galsworthy's generally wise, benign fathers who help to
produce tolerant and moral sons, Bowen presents smug
and self-righteous mothers, whose adherence to convention, hard and ferocious or lethally gentle as the
case may be, cuts off dimensions of experience and
emotion for their children. Although persuasive examples of these inhibiting and denying mothers exist
in both *The House in Paris* and *The Death of the
Heart,* the most disastrous mother, and the one Bowen
most fiercely satirizes, is the woman in *The Heat of
the Day,* who is so insulated by her comfortable home
and triviality (her morality is her endless insistence,
while denying all human interchange, that she find the
three pennies to give a visitor who will post a letter

for her back in London), so without love or feeling, that she can bring up a son who finally hates the past violently and is willing to betray his country during World War II. This treatment of generations indicates another difference between Galsworthy's historical attitude and that of Elizabeth Bowen. For Galsworthy, morality is represented—however imperfectly—in civilization, in the accumulated experience of England, which, although it requires further enlargement and concern, ought not be brushed aside or overturned. For Bowen, however, at least in her novels up until World War II, recent civilization often acts as a pressure of impacted conventionality that the moral person needs to pierce through in order to find a historical locus for wider and more genuine emotions. Neither author, however, sees a core of human feeling as primal or universal. For both, human possibility is best represented somewhere on a historical continuum, somewhere within the record of determining personal and social, although strictly human, relationships.

With *The Heat of the Day,* her novel set during and permeated by World War II, Bowen's fiction began to change markedly. In that novel, the focus is almost equally divided between a heroine much like Bowen's earlier ones and a young woman from the lower classes who survives the war through her complete lack of any sense of time or morality. And later novels continue the skepticism, the point of view that memory and conscience are delusions dependent on a particular middle-class ethos. *The Little Girls,* for example, shows the futility, from a distance of almost fifty years, of an attempt to dig out a meaningful past. And *Eva Trout,* Bowen's last novel, centers on a clumsy, over-sized woman who wanders about unable to find any role or function in the modern world. The character, Eva

Trout, is a metaphor, represents a sense of life, large, awkward, always out of kilter, unable to find a form. And the world surrounding the sense of life is also puzzling and indefinable: on the one hand, it is full of minute and trivial forms, conventions; on the other hand, it's chaotic, unpredictable, and violent. Life still exists, but the world has no place for it. For Bowen, in the later fiction, assimilation is reduction, richness is chaos and violence. Morality has come to seem, in *Eva Trout,* a luxury the characters cannot even imagine. World War II seems to mark a change in focus for a number of novelists of Bowen's generation. Evelyn Waugh, for example, shifted away from the metaphysical and historical certainties that lie behind his fierce satire in the early work toward a more open, far less metaphysically committed, consideration of ethical responses to experience in his brilliant trilogy about the war, now called *Sword of Honour.*

For many novelists of a later generation whose careers began during or after World War II, an ethical perspective as central to the fiction developed in a very different way. These writers began by assuming no metaphysical certainty, no universal core. Angus Wilson, widening his area of concern from the initial sharp vignettes and formal dependence on literary models, has, in novels like *No Laughing Matter,* increasingly seen the world, both before and after World War II, from a point of view sensitive to all the implications of personal, professional, and political fascism. And Saul Bellow, after the intensity of his early psychological studies of isolated man, like *Dangling Man* and *The Victim,* has focused on the ethical question of how the intelligent man with a consciousness of history, like the central figures of *Herzog* and *Mr. Sammler's Planet, ought* to live in the contemporary world. The resolutions of the novels are more difficult, more tenuous and qualified, than such brief listings can even suggest, but these writers ask questions that assume direct and concerned involvement in an uncertain world, in a metaphysical void. Another such novelist, more relentlessly and perhaps more philosophically speculative than the others, is Iris Murdoch. Her early novels—full of bizarre, comic incident and sudden switches in relationship (her characters always switch beds with a rapidity that indicates the tenuous and fragile quality she sees as underlying almost all human relationships)—are primarily existential statements. Characters fabricate abstractions or codes, intellectual or emotional, by which they try to live, and the abstraction invariably turns around and batters or destroys them. All that is left is a kind of creatureness, an unformulated sense of life, an existence. In some of these earlier novels, like *The Flight from the Enchanter,* Murdoch shows an ethical preference (and it is more on the level of preference than that of judgment or perspective) for those characters who escape enchantment, who, potential victims of the abstractions of others, will try not to victimize, bully, or impose themselves on others; but novels like *A Severed Head* seem almost to reverse the preference and to show in all the imagery attached to Honor Klein, the sense of strength and sharpness cutting through the fogs of unexamined complacency, a preference for the character who engages life even if by imposition. In both instances, these preferences are buried in a world in which ethical consciousness is generally self-defeating, and only those content simply to exist can survive. In her sixth novel, *An Unofficial Rose,* however, the ethical dimension becomes more important. Not only are ethical questions, like what is good, asked centrally, but also the resolution of the novel does not sanction unconsciousness. Rather, in terms appropriate to a novel in which the cultivation of roses is a central metaphor, the good characters define themselves in terms of "unofficial" forms, rich, floral, yet individual and ethical shapes to experience.

Murdoch publishes novels so frequently (fourteen in the last eighteen years) that changes in direction or focus are not visible, in any linear progression, from one novel to the next. Rather, direction seems to change over a group of novels: a theme is announced, complicated, reversed, seen with a different tone from a different perspective, finally more fully resolved. To look at Murdoch's fiction in this way introduces the possible critical fallacy of assuming a more certain formulation in the most recent novel, of developing a critical point of view that looks at her past novels retrospectively and charts complex movements toward a fixed present. All this may be upset or modified by the next novel she publishes. Nevertheless, I see a gradual direction in the fiction from the existential to the ethical. The group after *An Unofficial Rose* suspends and complicates (or, sometimes, turns about) the partially ethical themes, as *The Unicorn* makes the problems more complex by adding dimensions of mystery and myth, and *The Red and the Green* transfers the issues into a specifically political setting: Dublin just before the Easter uprising of 1916. For these novels, the ethical issues revolve around a debate concerning freedom and imprisonment, the complications involved between the extremes of letting others alone and, in one way or another, intellectually or emotionally, controlling their conduct.

In Murdoch's four most recent novels, *The Nice and the Good, Bruno's Dream, A Fairly Honourable De-*

feat, and *An Accidental Man,* the ethical framework
provides a fairly consistent structure, a central debate
and resolution worked through the usual Murdoch
world of bizarre incident and predictably unpredictable
encounters. In two of these novels, *The Nice and the
Good* and *A Fairly Honourable Defeat,* the debate
contrasts a false morality with a genuine one by establishing a married couple who think their relationship
a model for others. In one novel, Murdoch satirizes
their hollowness; in the other, she introduces an agent
of evil, impelled by his own isolation and pain, who
destroys them. Often, in these novels, the false, the
smug, and the self-righteous are articulate about their
pretended virtues; they theorize and erect structures
that delude themselves and others. But those posed
against them, the genuinely good, are not the unconscious creatures of the earlier novels; rather, more
quietly, less grandiosely, they both articulate and act
out their ethics, their concern for others, their capacity
to see and act in terms of the self and other selves and
of individual human particularities. God figures, too,
are not simply the deluding myths of the early novels,
for God figures, given their supernatural powers and
status only by themselves or other human beings, have
the humanly ethical choice between involving themselves in human concerns and judgments and remaining
remote in the enclosures of human fabrication. The
unconscious characters, on the other hand, are, in the
later fiction, likely to be characterized as "accidental,"
exercising no will, following random personal impulse,
and living as harmful parasites.

Murdoch's attitude toward human efforts to achieve
meaning and worth consciously have changed considerably during her career as a novelist. Almost all the
early novels, like *The Sandcastle* and *The Bell,* con-

tained a comic engineering feat of great ingenuity and complexity that was invariably futile. In the later novels, as a development from the treatment of freedom and imprisonment in the middle novels, human efforts to propel others are represented by interference, by one character acting to save or instruct or impose himself on another. And Murdoch's attitude toward interference is complex. Sometimes, interference is cruel and brutal, an immoral imposition; at other times, it is incompetent but warmhearted, leading to the ludicrous rather than to disaster. Some who theorize too much and too consistently, interfere in the wrong way at the wrong time, violate, in their inconsistent attempts at consistency, both themselves and others; some interfere only as a projection of themselves, with no recognition of the other. Yet some interference is genuinely relevant to others, is good. As one of the characters says, "separated" help is possible, help that recognizes both others and the self and that genuinely communicates across the space between separate human identities. For Murdoch, interference can help or hurt, be ethical or not; but, because it consists so entirely of relationships with others, it establishes a clear and convenient means for defining the ethical possibilities within a situation. Characters reveal themselves through the quality of their impositions, their deliberate and conscious connections with other people.

The ethical novel is itself an interference, a deliberate and structured imposition, an assault, perhaps, on our conventional simplicities or too easy assurances about human behavior. In "Mr. Bennett and Mrs. Brown," it was just this quality in the fiction of the Edwardians that seemed to anger Woolf most: "Sometimes I wonder if we are right to call them books at all. For they leave one with so strange a feeling of incompleteness and dissatisfaction. In order to complete them it seems necessary to join a society, or, more desperately, to write a cheque." [12] In one sense, Woolf's comment is snide and reductive, the measure of a kind of aristocratic remoteness. Yet, metaphorically, the statement is accurate, for the fiction of the Edwardians, like that with an ethical focus, does relate to experience, does shape and comment on issues in such a way that readers, although they seldom respond quite so literally as Woolf suggests, often bring the fiction into their own experience. Fiction with an ethical focus invites participation and asks, in its dependence on prescriptive judgments, the reader for a kind of assent that reflects, with some degree of directness, his not exclusively literary experience. We probably do not, when involved in and convinced by this kind of novel, immediately sign on the dotted line of virtue; we do, however, sometimes consider or reconsider actions of our own that come near the terms of the fiction.

In her fiction, Iris Murdoch, apparently quite consciously, recognizes that her kind of novel is a form of interference. The plots, the elaborate structures overturned, the human pretensions made comic—all interfere with settled abstract versions of experience. And she has defended this perspective, this role of serious literature in modern society, in a speech to the American Academy of Arts and Letters:

Great art, especially literature, but the other arts too, carries a built-in self-critical recognition of its incompleteness. It accepts and celebrates jumble, and the bafflement of the mind by the world. The incomplete pseudo-object, the work of art, is a lucid commentary upon itself. . . .

. . . Words constitute the ultimate texture and

stuff of our moral being, since they are the most
refined and delicate and detailed, as well as the most
universally used and understood of the symbolisms
whereby we express ourselves into existence. We
became spiritual animals when we became verbal
animals. The *fundamental* distinctions can only be
made in words. Words are spirit. Of course eloquence
is no guarantee of goodness, and an inarticulate
man can be virtuous. But the quality of a civilization
depends upon its ability to discern and reveal truth,
and this depends on the scope and purity of its
language.[13]

She then challenged the idea that the study of science
might ever substitute for the study of literature: "But
the study of a language or a literature or any study that
will increase and refine our ability to *be* through words
is part of a battle for civilization and justice and freedom, for clarity and truth, against vile fake-scientific
jargon and spiritless slipshod journalese and tyrannical
mystification. There are not two cultures. There is only
one culture and words are its basis; words are where
we live as human beings and as moral and spiritual
agents." [14] Over fifty years, several degrees of philosophical sophistication, and very different interests in
terms of the technique of the novel separate John
Galsworthy from Iris Murdoch. Yet their sense of the
importance of literature, of the relationship between
literature and history, and of the novel's focus on ethics
and immediacy brings them, fundamentally, quite
close together.

In its immediacy, its willingness to comment directly
on problems in human experience, the novel with an
ethical focus is vulnerable. It risks sentimentality or
banality, the simple duplication of experience we call

soap opera. At times, as in the opening twenty pages of *A Fairly Honourable Defeat,* the simple dialogue between two characters, announcing all the themes and introducing all the other characters, seems very close to the kind of soap opera it is probably intended to parody. But the difference between fiction with an ethical focus and much soap opera (like the difference between some soap operas and others) is a difference in intelligence and range, a difference in the kinds of ethical commentary offered implicitly and explicitly. The immediacy of this kind of fiction requires directness; and the ethical focus requires judgment—so that the writer cannot defend himself against possible banality or sentimentality by distance or methodology. *What* he shows is his only defence; the intelligence, the range, the quality of his ethical commentary is his principal distinction. And his position is vulnerable because his ethics are human, because, in any absolute sense, he never knows whether or not what he is saying is true. If the closeness of this kind of novel gains a possible immediacy, it also risks immediate dissent and excessively literal response. In addition, the novel with an ethical focus can easily force incident into apparent melodrama, for to extend the range and possible consequences of an ethical example within the context of verisimilitude is to court the dangers of the Aristotelean improbable-possible. Yet possibility, the range of human experience itself, is just as worthy a subject as probability—the typical, the abstracted. At least, so it has seemed to a number of distinguished twentieth-century novelists.

Since it is so immediate, so closely connected with life, the novel with an ethical focus is also, as both Woolf and Murdoch indicated, incomplete. It invites comparison with life, continuity in terms of the reader's experience, but sometimes also confusion and the incapacity to take resolutions as far as the implications of the questions go. It lacks the ringing assertion of fiction with the kind of vision or certainty that Virginia Woolf called for; it lacks the satisfaction of finality. Part of the appeal of Woolf's perspective is the authority of its eloquence or, rather, the eloquence of its authority, its assurance of finality. Although I can envy and admire this, there is another appeal in fiction that, for some of us, is just as powerful: the appeal to closeness and to differences, to what we might have been or might be or might become, to what is self and what is not self, to all the absolute questions we ask and partial answers we find. And this kind of appeal, which does not demand completeness, can be shaped and realized through fiction with a human and ethical focus.

Notes

1. Virginia Woolf, "Mr. Bennett and Mrs. Brown," reprinted in *The Captain's Death Bed and Other Essays* (New York: Harcourt, Brace, 1950), p. 119.

2. Ibid., pp. 109–110.

3. Arnold Bennett, *The Journals of Arnold Bennett, 1896–1910,* ed. Newman Flower (London: Cassell and Company, 1932), p. 308.

4. Calvin Bedient, *Architects of the Self* (Berkeley: University of California Press, 1972), p. 30.

5. E. M. Forster, *Aspects of the Novel* (New York: Harcourt, Brace, 1927), p. 63.

6. H. V. Marrot, *The Life and Letters of John Galsworthy* (New York: Charles Scribner's Sons, 1936), pp. 114–115.

7. John Galsworthy, *End of the Chapter* (London: Heinemann, 1935), p. 204.

8. John Galsworthy, *The Forsyte Saga* (London: Heinemann, 1922), p. 748.

9. John Galsworthy, *A Modern Comedy* (London: Heinemann, 1929), p. 735.

10. Ibid., p. xv.

11. Galsworthy, *End of the Chapter,* p. 764.

12. Woolf, "Mr. Bennett and Mrs. Brown," p. 105.

13. Iris Murdoch, Blashfield Address, delivered to the American Academy of Arts and Letters, May 17, 1972. Reprinted as "Salvation by Words," in *New York Review of Books,* June 15, 1972, p. 4.

14. Ibid., p. 5.

THREE

Fiction and Repetition: *Tess of the d'Urbervilles*

J. Hillis Miller

> Considérons les deux formules: "seul ce qui se res-
> semble diffère," "seules les différences se ressem-
> blent." Il s'agit de deux lectures du monde dans la
> mesure où l'une nous convie à penser la différence
> à partir d'une similitude ou d'une identité préalables,
> tandis que l'autre nous invite au contraire à penser
> la similitude et même l'identité comme le produit
> d'une disparité de fond. La première définit exacte-
> ment le monde des copies ou des représentations;
> elle pose le monde comme icône. La seconde, contre
> la première, définit le monde des simulacres. Elle pose
> le monde lui-même comme phantasme. (Gilles
> Deleuze, *Logique du sens,* p. 302) *

MEANING in any work of literature derives, in part,
from the repetition of elements within the work or by

the repetition by elements within the work of something outside the work. This "something outside" may be literary or extraliterary. In a work of literature what is said two times or more is likely to be important. Repetition is a major device, especially in long works like a novel or a narrative poem, to call attention to an element, to encourage the reader to notice the element, to focus his attention on it, and to attempt to identify its meaning. The first instance of the color red in *Tess of the d'Urbervilles* may be passed over as trivial or as merely representational. (It is not unlikely that Tess would have a red ribbon in her hair.) When the reader encounters the third, the fourth, and the fifth red things, however, red begins to stand out as a salient motif, repeated in sequence, like those words Tess meets on walls or fences painted by the itinerant religious man, each word oddly followed by a comma: "THY, DAMNATION, SLUMBERETH, NOT," or "THOU, SHALT, NOT, COMMIT, . . ."

The role of repetition as a generator of meaning in literature is taken for granted in most forms of criticism. Moreover, it is for the most part taken for granted that by repetition one means "repetition with a difference." Each recurring motif or element comes back in a changed form each time, even if that difference is only a matter of an alteration in the surrounding and defining context. In spite of the general consensus on these matters, however, the workings of repetition in literature remain extremely problematic. This essay is an attempt to identify some of the problems, particularly as they arise in connection with the reading of narrative fiction.

My example is *Tess of the d'Urbervilles,* a novel especially rich in the texture of its repetitions and in the diverse forms these repetitions take. It is also a good text for such an investigation because the question of repetition is thematic in the novel. *Tess of the d'Urbervilles* is structured around manifold repetitions—recurrences verbal, thematic, and narrative. At the same time, it is a story about repetition. The way this is the case might be expressed by saying that the story of Tess poses a question, "Why is it that Tess is 'destined' to live a life which both exists in itself as the repetition of the same event in different forms and at the same time repeats the previous experience of others in history and in legend?" The question on the methodological level might be phrased by asking not why literary texts tend to be structured around various forms of repetition, but "What concept of repetition in general, in a given case, will allow the reader to control, understand, or interpret a text made up of a fabric of recurrences?" Another way to put this question is to ask: "What, in a given case, is the appropriate concept of difference? Are the differences between one example of a motif and another accidental or essential?"

The concept or question of repetition has had in modern times, in fact in the Western tradition generally from Plato onward, a considerable resonance. One thinks, in this connection, of Vico; of Kierkegaard's *Repetition;* of the theme of the eternal return in Nietzsche; of Freud's conception of the compulsion to repeat; of Mircea Eliade's focus on the function of the eternal return in archaic cultures; of the "Ouverture" to Claude Lévi-Strauss's *Le Cru et le cuit;* of the interest, in modern anthropology generally, in the differential repetition of myths; of the renewal of cyclical theories of history in Matthew Arnold or in Yeats; of the role of repetition in Heidegger's theory of time; of repetition in Proust and Mallarmé; of Gilles Deleuze's *Différence et répétition;* of an admirable essay by Eugène Vinaver on the role of repetition in medieval narrative, especially in the Arthurian cycle ("The Poetry of Interlace," in *The Rise of Romance*); of the discussion by A. J. Greimas of redundancy in literature and of the way it establishes what he calls a second-level code. Finally, there is a recent critical book by Bruce F. Kawin, *Telling It Again and Again: Repetition in Literature and Film* (Cornell, 1972), though Kawin seems to me to have the temporal structure involved in repetition exactly backward, seeing it as a principle of plenitude and presence rather than, as Mallarmé described it in "Mimique," a principle that develops what he calls "une apparence fausse de présent." Though I am not unmindful of these august contexts and am assuming them as a kind of penumbra around my more narrow focus, my purpose here is a humbly inductive investigation, as much as possible without theoretical presuppositions, of the role of repetition in *Tess of the d'Urbervilles.*

A number of distinctly different forms of repetition may be identified in *Tess.* One is the small-scale recurrence of verbal elements: words, figures of speech, shapes, or gestures; or there are, even more subtly, covert repetitions that act like metaphors, as the cigar-smoking Alec d'Urberville is said to be "the blood-red ray in the spectrum of [Tess's] young life," [1] while the sun's rays coming into her room in a later episode are said to look like that phallic-shaped garden flower (Kniphofia), called "red-hot poker" (p. 109). A second form of repetition in the novel is the large-scale duplication within the text of events or scenes, as Tess's life is made up of reenactments of the "same" event involving the same cluster of motifs: somnolence, the color red, some

act of violence done or received. A third form of repetition is the recurrence of motifs from one plot or
character to another within the same text, as 'Liza-Lu,
Tess's sister, seems at the end of the novel destined to
reenact another version of Tess's life. Another form is
the repetition by the character of previous generations,
or of historical or mythological characters, as Tess's violation repeats the violence done to long-dead peasant girls
by Tess's male ancestors, or as her death repeats the cru-
cifixion of Christ or the prehistorical sacrifices performed
at Stonehenge. Another kind of repetition is the recurrence in this novel of motifs, themes, characters, or events
from other novels by Hardy. Another is the way in
which narration is a repetition of past events. Within the
fiction of the novel, the narrator's storytelling is presented as his repetition in language of events that have
already happened, "out there" in the objective or
nonlinguistic world. The novel is usually interpreted
by its critics as a mirroring, as the repeating in a fictional
form of objective historical or sociological conditions
of nineteenth-century rural England, for example, the
displacement of the peasantry and the effects of the
introduction of modern farm machinery. In one way
or another mimesis is repetition. Any realistic theory of
fiction is a theory of repetition. The novel is also repeated by its title, by its subtitle, by the epigraph, and
by its sequence of four prefaces, or explanatory notes.
These prefaces discuss the way the novel and its subtitle
are repetitions. *Tess of the d'Urbervilles,* says Hardy
in the note to the first edition, is "an attempt to give
artistic form to a true sequence of things" (p. xv). "To
exclaim illogically against the gods, singular or plural,"
he says in the preface to the fifth edition, "is not such
an original sin of mine as he [Andrew Lang, who had
attacked the novel] seems to imagine" (p. xix). The

novel, then, is the repetition of an older sin, Shakespeare's sin in *King Lear,* or the historical Gloucester's
sin before that. In another of the prefaces, that of 1912,
he says the subtitle, "A Pure Woman / Faithfully presented by / Thomas Hardy," "was appended at the
last moment, after reading the final proofs, as being the
estimate left in a candid mind of the heroine's character"
(pp. xx–xxi). The subtitle was a summary of the
whole, another form of duplication. The prefaces, if
they call attention to the way the book is a repetition,
are also paradoxically in themselves reaffirmations of
the novel, attempts to efface it or to apologize for it,
which in that apology reiterate it or admit that once it
is written it cannot be erased, as, within the fiction,
Tess's life, once it has happened, can never not have
been. "The pages," says Hardy, writing of the preface
to the fifth edition, "are allowed to stand for what they
are worth, as something once said; but probably they
would not have been written now" (p. xx). In the act
of saying, "I would not write them now," in effect he
writes them over again. In the last prefatory note,
speaking of the subtitle, he says *"Melius fuerat non
scribere.* But there it stands" (p. xxi). Once more, in
saying, "I wish I had not said it," he says it again. The
proofreader's delete sign turns into a "stet."

Tess of the d'Urbervilles is a complex tissue of repetitions within repetitions, repetitions linked in chain
fashion to other repetitions, repetitions making up the
internal structure of the text, repetitions determining
its multiple relations to what is outside it: the author's
consciousness or life, other works by Hardy, social or
historical reality, other works by other authors, elements
from the mythological or fabulous past, and elements
from the purported past of the characters that have
occurred before the book begins. In order to try to

investigate more narrowly the way these various forms
of repetition work, I shall concentrate on the interpretation of a single important passage in the text, a
passage in which many of these forms of repetition
are both operative and overtly thematized, put explicitly
before the reader as problems. This is the passage
describing the violation of Tess. To call it either a rape
or a seduction would be to beg the fundamental questions that the book raises: the questions of the meaning
of Tess's experience and of its causes. Here is the
passage.

D'Urberville stooped; and heard a gentle regular
breathing. He knelt and bent lower, till her breath
warmed his face, and in a moment his cheek was
in contact with hers. She was sleeping soundly, and
upon her eyelashes there lingered tears.

Darkness and silence ruled everywhere around.
Above them rose the primeval yews and oaks of The
Chase, in which were poised gentle roosting birds
in their last nap; and about them stole the hopping
rabbits and hares. But, might some say, where was
Tess's guardian angel? where was the providence of
her simple faith? Perhaps, like that other god of
whom the ironical Tishbite spoke, he was talking, or
he was pursuing, or he was in a journey, or he was
sleeping and not to be awaked.

Why it was that upon this beautiful feminine
tissue, sensitive as gossamer, and practically blank
as snow as yet, there should have been traced such a
coarse pattern as it was doomed to receive; why so
often the coarse appropriates the finer thus, the
wrong man the woman, the wrong woman the man,
many thousand years of analytical philosophy have
failed to explain to our sense of order. One may,

indeed, admit the possibility of a retribution lurking in the present catastrophe. Doubtless some of Tess d'Urberville's mailed ancestors rollicking home from a fray had dealt the same measure even more ruthlessly towards peasant girls of their time. But though to visit the sins of the fathers upon the children may be a morality good enough for divinities, it is scorned by average human nature; and it therefore does not mend the matter.

As Tess's own people down in those retreats are never tired of saying among each other in their fatalistic way: "It was to be." There lay the pity of it. An immeasurable social chasm was to divide our heroine's personality thereafter from that previous self of hers who stepped from her mother's door to try her fortune at Trantridge poultry-farm. (Pp. 90–91)

I have said that this passage describes Tess's violation. The event is, however, as one can see, not described at all, or at any rate it is not described directly. It exists in the text only as a blank space, like Tess's "beautiful feminine tissue . . . practically blank as snow as yet." It exists as the gap between paragraphs in which the event has not yet occurred and those that see it as already part of the irrevocable past. If it is described in the text at all, it is described in oblique form. It exists in the text as a metaphor. Doubtless Hardy was not free to describe such a scene literally. One remembers in this connection the notorious fact that, in the first periodical version of *Tess,* in *The Graphic,* Hardy had to have Angel Clare wheel Tess and the other girls across a puddle in a wheelbarrow rather than carry them across in his arms. Even so, the effacement of the actual moment of Tess's loss of virginity, its vanishing from the text, is significant and functional. It is matched by the similar failure to describe directly all the crucial acts of violence that echo Tess's violation before and after its occurrence: the killing of the horse, Prince, when Tess falls asleep at the reins; the murder of Alec; the execution of Tess. None of these events is described literally. Death and sexuality, those two fundamental realities—events that seem to be present or actual when they happen, if any events are present and actual— happen in *Tess* only offstage, beyond the margin of the narration. They exist in the text only in displaced expressions, like that gigantic ace of hearts on the ceiling, which is the sign that Alec has been murdered, or the distant raising of the black flag which is the sign that Tess has been hanged.

The "sign" in the text of Tess's violation, the metaphor that is its indirect presence in Hardy's language, has, however, a deeper significance than those of the more straightforward ace of hearts or black flag. Tess's rape or seduction exists in the novel in a metaphor of the act of the "tracing" of a coarse pattern on Tess's flesh. This metaphor belongs to a chain of figures of speech in the novel that includes, along with the tracing of a pattern, the making of a mark, the carving of a line or sign, and the act of writing itself. Writing and the making of a trace are, for example, associated in the poem, "Tess's Lament," which, like the prefaces and the subtitle, says the novel again in a different way. "I cannot bear my fate as writ," says Tess in the poem, "I'd have my life unbe; / Would turn my memory to a blot, / Make every relic of me rot, / My doings be as they were not, / And gone all trace of me!" [2] All the elements in this chain of metaphors in one way or another involve a physical act that changes a material substance, marking it or inscribing something on it, so that it becomes no longer simply itself but the sign of something absent, something that has already happened, a "relic" or "trace." The metaphor of the tracing of a pattern has a multiple significance. It assimilates the real event to the act of writing about it. It defines both the novel and the events it presents as repetition, as the tracing of a pattern that already exists. Tess's violation exists, both when it "first" happens and in the narrator's telling, as the reenactment of an event that has already occurred. The physical act itself is the making of a mark, the outlining of a sign. This deprives the event of any purely present existence and makes of it an emblem referring backward and forward to a long chain of similar events throughout history. Tess's violation repeats the violence her mailed ancestors did to the peasant girls of their time; and, in another place in the novel, Tess does not want to learn about history "because," as she says, "what's the use of learning that I'm one of a long row only—finding out that there is set down in some old book somebody just like me, and to know that I shall act her part; making me sad, that's all. The best is not to remember that your nature and your past doings have been just like thousands' and thousands'; and that your coming life and doings'll be like thousands' and thousands' " (p. 162).

To sex and murder must be added writing. All three involve an act of cutting or piercing, which is paradoxical. It is the creation of a gap or division, as "an immeasurable social chasm was to divide our heroine's personality thereafter from that previous self of hers," or as her given name means "the reaper." At the same time, this event is the creation of a pattern that makes the present act only the reenactment of something that has happened innumerable times before, so depriving it of any purely present reality. "For nothing can be

sole or whole / That has not been rent." The other
meaning of Tess's name, "carrying ears of corn," suggests the paradoxical connection of division with
continuity or reproduction.[3]

All three versions of this paradox in *Tess*—sex,
murder, and writing—converge in the multiple implications of the metaphor of grafting used overtly and
covertly to describe the relation of Tess and Alec. The
metaphor is overt when the narrator says that, though
the spurious Stoke-d'Urbervilles were not "of the true
tree," nevertheless, "this family formed a very good
stock whereon to regraft a name which sadly wanted
such renovation" (p. 43); or when Tess's father says
of Alec, "sure enough he mid have serious thoughts
about improving his blood by linking on to the old
line" (p. 53); or when her mother says, "as one of the
genuine stock, she ought to make her way with 'en,
if she plays her trump card aright" (p. 61). The metaphor of grafting is present covertly, according to a
characteristically complex conjunction of motifs, when
the rapid ride Tess takes with Alec in the dog cart, the
ride that leads to Alec giving her "the kiss of mastery"
(p. 65), is described in the metaphor of a splitting
stick: "The aspect of the straight road enlarged with
their advance, the two banks dividing like a splitting
stick; one rushing past at each shoulder" (p. 63). Here
come together the association of rapid motion with
the sexual attraction between Alec and Tess and the
use of Tess's progress along the roads of Wessex as an
emblem of her journey through life. Those roads are
inscribed in ancient lines on the once virgin countryside,
as an inscription is traced out on a blank page. Both
Tess's journeys and the roads themselves are versions
of the paradox of a cutting, which is also the establishment of a new continuity, as a stick must be split to be

grafted or linked on to a new shoot. The "kiss of mastery" that anticipates Alec's sexual possession of Tess is "imprinted" (p. 64), as though it were a design stamped with a die, and Tess tries to undo the kiss by "wiping the spot on her cheek that had been touched by his lips" (p. 65), as though it were a mark left on her cheek. The word *graft,* it may be remembered, is linked to the word *graph* by way of their common ancestry in a word meaning carving, cutting, or inscribing. To this may be associated another word meaning a traced or carved-out sign, *hieroglyph.* This word is used in the novel to describe Tess's naïve expectation that she will see in Alec d'Urberville "an aged and dignified face, the sublimation of all the d'Urberville lineaments, furrowed with incarnate memories representing in hieroglyphic the centuries of her family's and England's history" (p. 45).

One final version of this motif has already been encountered in the passages about Alec as the "blood-red ray in the spectrum of [Tess's] young life," and about the sun's rays as "like red-hot pokers." The sun is in this novel, as in tradition generally, the fecundating male source, a principle of life, but also a dangerous energy able to pierce and destroy, as Tess, at the end of the novel, lying on the stone of sacrifice at Stonehenge, after her brief period of happiness with Angel, is wakened, just before her capture, by the first rays of the morning sun, which penetrate under her eyelids: "Soon the light was strong, and a ray shone upon her unconscious form, peering under her eyelids and waking her" (p. 505). This association of death and sexuality with a masculine sun had been prepared earlier in the novel, not only by the description of Alec as the blood-red ray in the spectrum of Tess's life, but also, most

explicitly, by the full context of that passage describing
the sun's rays as "like red-hot pokers":

> The sun, on account of the mist, had a curious
> sentient, personal look, demanding the masculine
> pronoun for its adequate expression. His present
> aspect, coupled with the lack of all human forms
> in the scene, explained the old time heliolatries in
> a moment. One could feel that a saner religion had
> never prevailed under the sky. The luminary was a
> golden-haired, beaming, mild-eyed God-like creature,
> gazing down in the vigour and intentness of youth
> upon an earth that was brimming with interest
> for him.
>
> His light, a little later, broke through chinks of
> cottage shutters, throwing stripes like red-hot pokers
> upon cupboards, chests of drawers, and other furni-
> ture within; and awakening harvesters who were
> not already astir. (P. 109)[4]

The coarse pattern inscribed on Tess's flesh is, the
reader assumes, traced out in red, and it should be clear
now what meaning the reader should ascribe to all
the chain of red things in the novel: the red ribbon in
Tess's hair; her mouth ("He [Angel] saw the red interior of her mouth as if it had been a snake's" [p. 217]);
those red lips with which she says the characteristic
"UR" sound of her dialect; the strawberry that Alec
forces her to eat (" 'I would rather take it in my own
hand.' 'Nonsense,' he insisted; and in a slight distress
she parted her lips and took it in" [p. 47]); the roses
that Alec gives her with which she pricks her chin; the
red scratches on her wrist in the reaping scene ("as
the day wears on its feminine smoothness becomes
scarified by the stubble, and bleeds" [p. 112]); the red

stains made on Tess's arms when, in an extraordinary
scene, she approaches closer under Angel's window,
fascinated by his harp playing, making her way through
"tall blooming weeds emitting offensive smells" ("She
went stealthily as a cat through this profusion of
growth, gathering cuckoo-spittle on her skirts, cracking
snails that were underfoot, staining her hands with
thistle-milk and slug-slime, and rubbing off on her
naked arms sticky blights which, though snow-white on
the apple-tree trunks, made madder stains on her skin"
[p. 158]); the red-painted signs that have already been
cited ("THY, DAMNATION, SLUMBERETH, NOT"); the
"piece of blood-stained paper, caught up from some
meat-buyer's dust heap," which "beat[s] up and down
the road," "too flimsy to rest, too heavy to fly away"
(p. 380), when Tess makes her abortive attempt to
appeal to Angel's parents after he has abandoned her;
the "scarlet oozing" from Alec's face after Tess has
struck him with her threshing glove, "heavy and thick
as a warrior's" (p. 422) (an ironic reminiscence of
the gloves of her "armed progenitors" [p. 422]); the
growing blot of blood on the ceiling, like "a gigantic
ace of hearts" (p. 488), when Alec has been murdered.
All these red things are signs, marks, or emblems made
by that creative and destructive energy underlying
events to which Hardy gave the name "Immanent
Will," which is incarnated in one form in the sun, but
also diffused or distributed in all those agents that
fecundate, destroy, or make signs in the triple chain of
recurrent acts—sex, murder, and writing—that organizes this novel.

The novel itself is defined in the prefaces as a mark
or sign imprinted on Hardy's mind, as a die strikes a
coin, and repeated or reinscribed in the words of the
text. The novel is, Hardy tells his readers, "an impres-

sion, not an argument" (p. xviii). Hardy has "writ[ten] down how the things of the world strike him" (p. xix), and the subtitle is "the estimate left in a candid mind of the heroine's character," a reenactment of the tracing of a coarse pattern on Tess's virgin flesh. Here "candid" matches "practically blank as snow," and "estimate" matches the "measure" dealt by Tess's ancestors to long-dead peasant girls and measured out again less ruthlessly to Tess by Alec. "Estimate" and "measure" suggest "ration," "proportion," or "logic" making a design, as a throw of the dice makes a pattern or as reproduction is the dissemination of a genetic code. The same cluster of motifs is repeated again in the epigraph for the novel from *Two Gentlemen of Verona.* There sex and writing, with a reversal of the usual polarities of male and female, are joined again in the image of Hardy's "bosom" as both a bed and a writing tablet on which is inscribed Tess's name and her story—no doubt in letters of scarlet: "Poor wounded name, my bosom as a bed / Shall lodge thee." It is in accord with the deep logic of these recurrent configurations of Hardy's language that the passage about the masculine sun is followed by a description of the reaping machine "whose two broad arms of painted wood" are "of all ruddy things that morning the brightest," as "the paint in which they were smeared, intensified in hue by the sunlight, imparted to them a look of having been dipped in liquid fire" (p. 109). Another passage concentrates all these elements in a single sentence: "The sun was so low on that short last afternoon of the year that it shone in through a small opening and formed a golden staff which stretched across to [Tess's] skirt, where it made a spot like a paint mark set upon her" (p. 277).

What I have said so far, by way of commentary,

interpretation, or unfolding of the passage about the tracing of a coarse pattern on Tess's flesh, will suggest a way to read this novel or, in fact, a way to read literary works in general. Each passage is a node, a point of intersection or focus, on which converge lines leading from many other passages in the novel and ultimately including them all. No passage has any particular priority over the others, in the sense of being more important or as being the "origin" or "end" of the others. The sun is not the chief or archetypal representative of the Immanent Will in the novel, for the Immanent Will exists only in its representatives. Any motif in *Tess of the d'Urbervilles* exists only in the examples of it, none of which has a sovereign explanatory function for the others. Moreover, the chains of connection or of repetition that converge on a given passage are extremely complex and diverse in nature, and no one of these chains has archeological or interpretative priority over the others.

A novel like *Tess of the d'Urbervilles* has an astonishing thematic or textual richness, a richness that may not be organized according to some hierarchical principle. The reader can only thread his way from one element to another, interpreting each as best he can in terms of the others. It is possible to distinguish chains of connection that are material elements in the text, like the red things; or metaphors, like the figures of grafting or of writing; or covert, often etymological, associations like the connection of grafting with writing or cutting; or thematic elements, like sexuality or murder; or conceptual elements, like the question of cause or the theory of history in the novel; or quasi-mythological elements, like the association of Tess with the harvest or the personification of the sun as a benign god. None of these chains, however, has priority over the others as the true explanation of the meaning of the novel. Each is a permutation of the others rather than a distinct realm of discourse, as the myth of the paternal sun is a version of the dangerous power of Alec d'Urberville.

Taken altogether, the elements form a system of mutually defining motifs, each of which exists as its relation to the others. The reader must execute a lateral dance of interpretation to explicate any given passage, without ever reaching, in this sideways movement, any passage that is chief, original, or originating, a sovereign principle of explanation. The image of a chain, row, or sequence is itself fundamental in the novel. Hardy defines the novel as "an attempt to give artistic form to a true sequence of things" (p. xxv). The novel calls attention to the pattern of linear sequence in the powerful emblematic effect of topography in the novel. This leads the reader to think of Tess's life as her journey through the series of places where she lives. The novel, moreover, is organized as a sequence of seasons. Tess in one place sees her life as "numbers of to-morrows just all in a line," each saying, "I'm coming! Beware of me! beware of me!" (p. 159). The motif of the series or line is in fact introduced in the opening description by Parson Tringham of the d'Urberville ancestors "at Kingsbere-sub-Greenhill: rows and rows of you in your vaults, with your effigies under Purbeck-marble canopies" (pp. 5–6).

More, however, needs to be said about the "description" of Tess's violation. My interpretation so far has suggested that the various chains of meaning that converge on this passage are all of elements congruent with one another, as all the red things seem to mean the same thing. In fact, this is not the case, and my passage brings to the surface in a number of ways the relation of chiasmus that structures the relation among the elements in a given chain in Hardy's novel. The relation among the links in a chain of meanings for Hardy is always repetition with a difference, and the difference is as important as the repetition.

The way in which Tess's violation repeats with a difference the previous events it duplicates is made clear by its relation to the various models of explanation, tentative interpretations, which are incorporated into the fabric of the description itself only to be rejected. The passage is a description with interpretations, but interpretations that cancel or annul themselves, partly by their incompatibility with one another, in a way entirely characteristic of Hardy. His novels are puzzling not because they contain no self-interpretative elements, but because they contain too many irreconcilable ones. Criticism has usually erred by seizing on one element in a given novel as the single and chief explanation of the meaning of what happens. Part of the importance of the passage I am discussing lies in the fact that it so explicitly raises the question put before the reader by the book as a whole: "Why? Why does Tess suffer so?" Various aspects of Hardy's way of presenting Tess's story keep this question insistently before the reader: the emphasis on its linear sequentiality, which implies, as always, a causal relation among the elements that follow one another; the incompatibility between what she wills and what happens; and the way in which her life, in spite of her intentions, both forms itself as a sequence of repetitions and makes as a whole a pattern that is a repetition of earlier fictional, historical, or mythological prototypes. The emergence of an unwilled or undesired pattern raises the question of its source or cause. What is the originating power that causes Tess's life to fall into a symmetrical design leading her step by step to her execution? "Why was it," as the novel poses this question, ". . . there should have been traced such a coarse pattern?"

The passage proposes and explicitly or implicitly rejects six possible answers to this question. The reason for the rejection in each case lies in the fact that, though the explanatory model is duplicated by what happens to Tess, it is duplicated in the form of an ironic reversal, a crisscross of the elements involved that invalidates the model as a straightforward explanatory cause.

The first of these models is the relation of Tess's experience to that story of the "curious legend of King Henry III's reign" about "the killing by a certain Thomas de la Lynd of a beautiful white hart which the King had run down and spared. This profanation was made the occasion of a heavy fine" (p. 10). The old killing had not happened in the same forest where Tess lost her virginity; but, by way of the association of both with "the primeval yews and oaks" that grow there, The Chase can be seen as a displacement of the Forest of White Hart. In Henry III's time, however, justice was done and the violation revenged. No champion comes forward to defend Tess or to punish her violator.

The second explanatory model is the connection between what happens to Tess and events in nonhuman nature. This connection is made in the passage through the repetition of the word *gentle.* Tess's "gentle regular breathing" is like the "gentle roosting birds in their last nap." Tess thinks she has, in yielding to Alec, broken a universal moral law, but in fact she has, as the narrator says, "been made to break an accepted social law, but no law known to the environment in which she fancied herself such an anomaly" (p. 108).

The third interpretative model is rejected even more decisively and with an even more bitterly ironic chiasmus. "But, might some say, where was Tess's guardian angel? where was the providence of her simple faith? Perhaps, like that other god of whom the ironical Tishbite spoke, he was talking, or he was pursuing, or he was in a journey, or he was sleeping and not to be awaked." Many scholars have shown how well Hardy knew the Bible. This is a good example of the way he used his knowledge. The passage just quoted not only rejects any interpretation of what happens to Tess by way of orthodox theology, while laying the ground for the irony in Angel Clare's name, but also through the biblical echo presents Tess's situation once more as a repetition with a difference, a duplication that makes of the anterior model no satisfactory explanation of what happens to her. Just as Angel's name might lead the reader to hope that he might serve as a human embodiment of Tess's missing guardian angel, while in fact he offers her no protection, so Tess's world is one entirely bereft of any providential presence. Things happen to her as they happen and are guided from behind the scenes by no divine designer. Tess in her simple faith is ironically in the position not of the traditional Christian or Old Testament believer in Jehovah, but in the position of those prophets of Baal whose impotent god could not answer their prayer for a magic fire under the sacrificial bullock. Those priests were savagely mocked by Elijah, "the ironical Tishbite": "And they took the bullock which was given them, and they dressed *it,* and called on the name of Baal from morning even until noon, saying, O Baal, hear us. But *there* was no voice, nor any that answered. And they leaped upon the altar which was made. And it came to pass at noon, that Elijah mocked them, and said, 'Cry aloud: for he *is* a god; either he is talking, or he is pursuing, or he is in a journey, *or* peradventure he sleepeth, and must be awaked.' And they cried aloud, and cut themselves after their manner with knives and lancets, till the blood gushed out upon them" (I Kings, 18:26–28). In the Old Testament narrative, Elijah's prayers are answered with a fire that consumes the sacrifice, but in Tess's world Christianity has replaced the worship of Baal as a belief in a God absent or dead. A modern-day Elijah, the text implies, would be as powerless as those impotent priests of Baal. In a context repeating in a new way the elements of fire, sacrifice, and an act of violence in which blood flows, Tess's violation repeats its biblical prototype with a reversal of all the Old Testament valences, offering the reader no hope of a biblical interpretation of Tess's experience.

The next interpretative model proposed is the Platonic one, by way of the reference to that myth in the *Symposium,* proposed by Aristophanes. Each person, according to the myth, wanders through life separated from another half of the other sex. If he could find his missing half, the two together would make a spherical, androgynous whole. Once again Hardy reverses his model. The Platonic one is reversed by the rejection of the idea of a primary unity that has been separated. For Hardy, a person is not initially identified with his opposite, but begins in separation and is never able to find the right time or place for a union with his counterpart. "In the ill-judged execution of the well-judged plan of things," says Hardy in a comment that acts as a gloss for this strand in the passage describing Tess's violation, "the call seldom produces the comer, the man to love rarely coincides with the hour for loving. Nature does not often say 'See!' to her poor creature at a time when seeing can lead to happy doing; or reply 'Here!'

to a body's cry of 'Where?' till the hide-and-seek has become an irksome, outworn game. . . . [I]n the present case, as in millions, it was not the two halves of a perfect whole that confronted each other at the perfect moment; a missing counterpart wandered independently about the earth waiting in crass obtuseness till the late time came. Out of which maladroit delay sprang anxieties, disappointments, shocks, catastrophes, and passing-strange destinies" (pp. 48–49).

The natural, legendary, biblical, and Platonic models are repeated with a difference or reversal of sign that makes of the relation between the model and its duplication no straightforward retracing of a pattern but a reversal of its implications. In the final such model, the passage at first seems to invite the reader to interpret Tess's experience according to a conventional idea of fate: whether this is the idea, expressed by Tess in "Tess's Lament," that a person's life is preinscribed in some book of fate, written out there, and only copied from a predetermined pattern in its actual living through, or whether it is the idea that there is a designing mind controlling Tess's actions and "dooming" her to follow a certain pattern in her life. Tess's virgin flesh is "doomed to receive" the trace of a "coarse pattern," and the pity of her life lies in the fact that "it was to be," according to the reading of it by her neighbors. By the time the reader has followed out the implications of the reversal of the other models proposed in the passage, however, he understands that Hardy's concept of fate cannot be dissociated from the notion of chance. Each crucial event in Tess's life is like a throw of the dice that creates the decisive configurations of her life—the chance encounter of Tess and Angel at the beginning; or the unlucky accident of the killing of Prince, which leads Tess to seek her family's fortune at Trantridge; or the chance encounter of Tess's father with Parson Tringham, which "originates" the whole sad sequence; or the unlucky chance that makes Tess's confessional letter slide under the rug in Angel's room, rather than reaching its intended destination. Each of these events is at once fated and accidental, like the mating of genes that creates a given individual. It happens by chance, as a fortuitous conjunction, but, as the sequence of such chances lengthens out to form a chain, it can in retrospect be seen to form a pattern of neatly repetitive events constituting Tess's destiny. The episodes of *Tess of the d'Urbervilles* take place in a line, each following the last. Ultimately they form a row traced out in time, just as Tess's course is traced across the roads of southern England. In the same way, Tess is herself only one of a long row of people who have had experiences like hers. Each episode in her life, as it occurs, adds itself to previous ones; and, as they accumulate, behold! they make a pattern, a design traced through time and on the landscape of England, like the prehistoric horses carved out on the chalk downs. Suddenly, to the retrospective eye of the narrator, of the reader, and ultimately even of the protagonist herself, the pattern is there. Each event, as it happens, is alienated from itself and swept up into the design. It ceases to be enclosed in itself and becomes a sign referring to previous and to later episodes, which are signs in their turn.

The second of Deleuze's formulations in my epigraph, it is clear, defines Hardy's concept of repetition. For Hardy, two elements or events do not repeat one another because they are both copied from some preexisting archetype or model; rather, resemblance or repetition arises spontaneously from the alignment of different events. Difference is constitutive of resemblance, rather than the other way around. Similitude arises from a "basic disparity" in the events that generate a design of repetition as each follows the others in a linear sequence.

Any providential or dooming supernatural mind is missing from Hardy's world. The Immanent Will is, as Hardy tells his readers in the forescene of *The Dynasts,* a drowsing knitter, who weaves the web of life by unconscious rote, like an automaton. Any event, like a chance throw of the dice, takes its place as soon as it occurs in a long line of similar throws. It thereby becomes a repetition, a repetition that seems in retrospect something that "was to be." Hardy's notion of fatality is the reflex of his notion of chance. Out of the "flux and reflux, the rhythm of change" that "alternate[s] and persist[s] in everything under the sky" (p. 447), emerges as if by miracle the pattern of repetitions in differences forming the design of Tess's life. Such repetitions produce similarity out of difference and are controlled by no center, origin, or end outside the chain of recurrent elements. For *Tess of the d'Urbervilles,* and perhaps for some other works of literature as well, this alternative to the traditional Platonic, metaphysical, or "centered" concept of repetition emerges as the way the text actually produces and affirms its meaning.

Here may be identified the meaning of the first half of Hardy's definition of the novel as "an attempt to give an artistic form to a true sequence of things." The artistic form is the novelist's interpretation of the events, an interpretation that does not falsify the events but imposes meaning on them by reading them in a certain way, as a sentence may have entirely different meanings depending on how it is read. The meaning is there and not there. It is a matter of position, of emphasis, of spacing, of punctuation. In the preface of

1892, Hardy recognizes the revolutionary effect such a new emphasis, reversing the usual positions of value, may have. To be led by a new "sentiment" of human worth or meaning to call the "impure" the "pure" may lead to a reversal of the usual relations of possession and dominance in society. The whole chain of family and social connections may be upset by something that begins in a passing impression. The adverse critics of *Tess,* said Hardy, "may have causes to advance, privileges to guard, traditions to keep going; some of which a mere tale-teller, who writes down how the things of the world strike him, without any ulterior intentions whatever, has overlooked, and may by pure [!] inadvertence have run foul of when in the least aggressive mood. Perhaps some passing perception, the outcome of a dream hour, would, if generally acted on, cause such an assailant considerable inconvenience with respect to position, interests, family, servant, ox, ass, neighbour, or neighbour's wife. . . . So densely is the world thronged that any shifting of positions, even the best warranted advance, galls somebody's kibe. Such shiftings often begin in sentiment, and such sentiment sometimes begins in a novel" (pp. xxix–xxx). In his quietly ironic way, Hardy, as the reader can see, is claiming a powerfully subversive effect for his novel. When by "pure inadvertence" he wrote the novel and summarized its impression on his candid mind by giving it the subtitle, "A Pure Woman / Faithfully Presented by / Thomas Hardy," he initiated a shifting of positions, like the altered emphasis on words in a sentence, which would, if acted on, ultimately rearrange the chain of power relationships in society.[5]

If the pattern and the meaning of the pattern emerge only through the sequence itself, a sequence in which each element adds itself as a differential repetition of the others, giving meaning to them as well as receiving meaning from them, then it is impossible to formulate any fixed meaning for the color red or for any other element in the text, just as it is impossible to find a "key passage" that will tell the reader what red "means." It means something different each time, but the meaning of each time is the relation of that time to the others. The meaning, moreover, comes into existence only in an act of interpretation, an act of spacing, punctuation, and emphasis. This act is performed by the characters, by the narrator, and by the reader. Attention is insistently called to it throughout the novel in the many examples of "false interpretation" that are "demystified" by the narrator: the comic example of the bull who thought it was Christmas Eve, or the more serious dramatization of Angel's infatuation with Tess and his interpretation of her as like Artemis or Demeter (p. 167), or the description of Tess's "idolatry" of Angel (p. 273), or Tess's false reading of nature as reproaching her for her impurity. All interpretation, however, is false interpretation in the sense that it is the picking out of similarities, the imposition of a pattern by a certain way of making cross connections between one sign and those that come before and after. Any interpretation is an artistic form given to the true sequence of things. This does not mean that the narrator or the reader is free to give the narrative any meaning he wishes, but that the pattern is subject to "free play," is formally "undecidable." Meaning emerges from a reciprocal act in which interpreter and what is interpreted both contribute to the making or the finding of a pattern, according to that principle of interpretation as both invention and discovery that Hardy defined in a passage in his autobiography: "As, in looking at a carpet, by following one colour a certain pattern is suggested, by following another colour, another; so in life the seer should watch that pattern among general things which his idiosyncrasy moves him to observe, and describe that alone. This is, quite accurately, a going to Nature; yet the result is no mere photograph, but purely [!] the product of the writer's own mind" (*The Life of Thomas Hardy* [London: Macmillan & Co., 1965], p. 153). To add a new interpretation to the interpretation already proposed by the author is to attach another link to the chain of interpretations, to take an impression in one's turn, to represent to oneself what already exists as a representation.

The saddest fact about *Tess of the d'Urbervilles* is that her wish to be "forgotten quite" ("Tess's Lament," line 1) cannot be fulfilled. She can die, but the traces of her life will remain, for example, in the book that records the impression she made on the narrator's imagination. Her life has a power of duplicating itself, which cancels her failure to have progeny, as in the life of her sister, which will be, beyond the end of the book, another repetition, with a difference, of the pattern of Tess's life. Beyond that, the reader comes to see, there will be another and then another, ad infinitum. If the novel is the impression made on Hardy's candid mind by Tess's story, the reader is invited to receive the impression again in his turn, according to that power of a work of art to repeat itself indefinitely to which the novel calls attention in a curious passage concerning Tess's sensitivity to music. Here is a final bit of evidence that Hardy saw the principle of repetition, in life as in art, as impersonal, immanent, and self-generating rather than as controlled by any external power. The "simplest music" has "a power over" Tess that can "wellnigh drag her heart out of her bosom at times" (p. 106).

She reflects on the strange coercive effect church music has on her feelings: "She thought, without exactly wording the thought, how strange and godlike was a composer's power, who from the grave could lead through sequences of emotion, which he alone had felt at first, a girl like her who had never heard of his name, and never would have a clue to his personality" (p. 107). *Tess of the d'Urbervilles,* as long as a single copy still exists, will have its strange and godlike power to lead readers through the sequences of emotions its pattern traces out.

Notes

* "Consider two formulas: 'only that which resembles itself differs,' 'only differences resemble one another.' It is a question of two readings of the world to the degree that one asks us to think of difference from the point of view of an initial similitude or identity, whereas the other invites us on the contrary to think of similitude and even of identity as the product of a basic disparity. The first exactly defines the world of copies or of representations; it establishes the world as icon. The second, against the first, defines the world of simulacra. It establishes the world itself as phantasm."

1. Thomas Hardy, *Tess of the d'Urbervilles,* Wessex ed. (London: Macmillan & Co., 1912), p. 47. Further citations from this novel will be from this edition and will be identified by page numbers in parentheses after quotations.

2. Thomas Hardy, *The Collected Poems* (London: Macmillan & Co., 1930), p. 162.

3. For these etymologies, see [Charlotte M. Yonge], *History of Christian Names* (London, 1863), I, 272, cited by Michael Millgate, *Thomas Hardy: His Career as a Novelist* (New York: Random House, 1971), pp. 219, 403. Millgate notes that this work was "the standard Victorian work on Christian names" and that Hardy owned a copy of the one-volume

edition of 1884, now in the Colbeck Collection of the University of British Columbia.

4. As Michael Millgate notes (*Thomas Hardy*, p. 403), Hardy probably read when it appeared Max Müller's essay, "Solar Myths," in *Nineteenth Century* 18 (December 1885): 900–922.

5. A parallel for Hardy's insight into the effect of "points" or of emphases in determining meaning is to be found in *A Midsummer-Night's Dream*, V, 1. (I am indebted to René Girard for calling my attention to this passage.) After Quince has said the correct words of the prologue, but with the pauses and emphases in the wrong places, so that it says the opposite of what its author meant, the gentle folk comment on his error:

Theseus. This Fellow does not stand upon points.

Lysander. He hath rid his prologue like a rough colt; he knows not the stop. A good moral, my lord: it is not enough to speak, but to speak true.

Hippolyta. Indeed he hath played on his prologue like a child on a recorder; a sound, but not in government.

Theseus. His speech was like a tangled chain; nothing impaired, but all disordered.

FOUR

D. H. Lawrence's Dualism: The Apollonian-Dionysian Polarity and *The Ladybird*

James C. Cowan

THE American novelist Henry Miller, in his fragment "Creative Death," describes D. H. Lawrence's work as "altogether one of symbol and metaphor," with a world view characterized by its dualism: "Phoenix, Crown, Rainbow, Plumed Serpent, all these symbols," Miller writes, "center about the same obsessive idea: *the resolution of two opposites in the form of a mystery.*" [1] Miller then proceeds briefly to relate Lawrence's dualism to Friedrich Nietzsche's concept of the dialectical processes of thought lying behind creative art, the opposing processes that Nietzsche denoted by the names of their classical prototypes as the Apollonian and Dionysian. For the moment, passing over the many individual and idiosyncratic differences with which the work of any imaginative writer, such as Lawrence, is concerned, I should like to explore Lawrence's characteristic way of perceiving the world by relating it more fully to these two broad intellectual and cultural traditions in western thought.

In his youthful manifesto, *The Birth of Tragedy* (1872), Nietzsche wrote: "A great deal will have been won for the science of aesthetics when we shall have succeeded in not merely recognizing intellectually, but directly and clearly seeing, that the development of art depends on the dual influence of Apollonian and Dionysian forces—as reproduction depends on the sexes, in their unrelenting conflict and only occasional—periodic —reconciliation." [2] Identifying the two Greek divinities of art as figures eloquently embodying the "great division, with respect to both source and aim, between the art of the sculptor, Apollonian art, and the non-pictorial art, music, of Dionysus," Nietzsche says: "The two impulses, different as they are, were carried along side by side, generally in open opposition, provoking each other to ever new, more mighty births through which to perpetuate the war of a pair of opposites that the shared word 'art' only apparently overbridges; until at last, through a metaphysical miracle of the Hellenic 'will,' the two were united, and in that pairing generated the art that was as Dionysian as Apollonian: Attic tragedy." [3]

In a subsequent figure, Nietzsche identifies these opposing forces with the separate physiological and aesthetic worlds of *dream*—in its pre-Freudian, Apollonian sense as a formal, pictorial given—and *intoxication,* in its Dionysian sense as inward, psychic experience. *Dream* in Nietzsche's usage, is analogous to the outer world of concrete perceptions ordered by spatial aesthetic relationships. *Intoxication,* on the other hand, is analogous to the inner world of psychic phenomena

involving temporal aesthetic relationships. The arts of
Apollo, as lord of light, "the glorious divine image of
the *principium individuationis* itself, in whose gesture
and glances the whole delight and wisdom of the
'world illusion' speaks to us," Nietzsche designates as
sculpture and epic poetry. The arts of Dionysus, as lord
of darkness, the divine image of the Eleusinian mysteries, are music, the dance, and lyric poetry. If Apollonian forces are at work in the rational and pictorial
qualities of these Dionysian arts, then Dionysian forces
are to be found, for example, in "the author's crafts-
manly concern for the musical effects of his prose, its
rhythms, verbal tones, and spheres of emotional association" as in leitmotivs.[4]

The Apollonian principle of individuation in consciousness involves the rational faculty of logical reason.
But what happens when, with horror, as Schopenhauer
describes it, the individual "suddenly finds himself in
error with respect to his interpretation of the forms of
appearance"—that is, "when the logic of causality . . .
seems to have been fractured by an exception"? Joseph
Campbell has observed: "The transition then is from
an aesthetic (Apollonian) to a properly religious
dimension of experience (or, in Nietzsche's terminology,
toward Dionysian rapture); and the sense of awe,
dread, or terror that is then experienced is something
different altogether from any 'kinetic,' natural loathing
or terror before an odious or dangerous object." What
happens, in short, is "a break in the tissue of temporal-
spatial-causal relationships," which results in the
"chilling . . . sense of the immediacy of something . . .
that is inconceivable," whether it be god, ghost, or
void.[5]

The immediate effect of this transport upon the
individual is, in other words, the sense of the *numinous*.

Rudolf Otto, in his theological study *The Idea of the Holy,* identifies "this experience of awe, of dread, as reciprocal to the Kantian *x,* the source and prime ingredient of religion—all religion: an experience *sui generis,* which is lost, however, when identified with the Good, the True, Love, Mercy, the Law, this conceptualized deity or that." The sense of the numinous cannot be taught; it can only be experienced.[6]

The subsequent effect of this transport upon society is the sense of unity in a higher commonality. As Nietzsche explains: "Under the magic of the Dionysian force, not only does the bond between man and man again close together, but alienated, hostile, or suppressed Nature celebrates her festival of reconciliation with her lost son, man. . . . With flowers and garlands is the car all strewn of Dionysus: in its span stride panther and tiger." Nietzsche gives Schiller's *Paean to Joy* in Beethoven's Ninth Symphony as an example: "Now each, in the Gospel of World Harmony, feels himself to be not only united with his neighbor, reconciled and blended, but one—as though the veil of māyā had been rent apart and now only fluttered in shreds around the mysterious primordial One. Mankind, singing, dancing, professes itself to be a member of a higher commonality."[7]

Despite this celebration of man's universal brotherhood, however, Nietzsche did not, as Walter Kaufmann observes, thereby endorse the Dionysian per se, but only the synthesis of this passion with the Apollonian "principle of individuation."[8] The Dionysian alone, far from being glorified, is pictured throughout as a "fever" that, left unchecked, led to "sexual licentiousness." As Nietzsche puts it, "precisely the most savage beasts of nature were unfettered here, to the point of that disgusting mixture of voluptuousness and cruelty

which always seemed to me the proper 'witches' brew."
Only the Apollonian principle of the Greeks could
"control this destructive disease, . . . harness the Dionysian flood, and . . . use it creatively." Thus, Nietzsche
is already moving toward that principle of synthesis
which, in his later works, would be called Dionysian.
As Kaufmann points out, the Dionysus who is the
opposite of Apollo in Nietzsche's first book is not the
same as that of the "Dionysus versus the Crucified" of
his last: "The later Dionysus is the synthesis of the two
forces which are represented by Dionysus and Apollo
in *The Birth of Tragedy*." [9]

In the earlier book, Nietzsche sets up two diamet-
rically opposed cultural traditions between which, at
this point, it should be possible to draw several generic
distinctions.

The Apollonian tradition, concerned with exterior
objects that occupy linear space or with externalized
mental conceptions, elevates as "real" that mode of
perception characterized by the objectifying intellect.
The ideal of intellectual beauty becomes, then, the
rational faculty, making analytical discriminations in
the conscious mind. In this mode, the intellectual seeker
detaches himself from the subjective to project himself
in quest of the light of truth in the outer world. This
tradition assumes a linear development in a causal
sequence to be described in discriminatory language—
as in the terminology of the sciences, social sciences,
and technology—with a fixed, definite, objective truth
as a reachable end point.

The Dionysian tradition, on the contrary, concerned
with interior perceptions, elevates as "real" that mode
of perception characterized by the creative imagination.
The ideal of intellectual beauty becomes, now, the
intuitive faculty, making synthesizing comparisons in

the creative unconscious. In this mode, the intellectual seeker incorporates elements of the outer world into the inner world, to seek the truth darkly by plunging into the cyclic night within the self. This tradition assumes a cyclic development in a recurrent pattern in which the intuitive perception of truth can never be described in discriminatory language but only, as in the writings of mystics and mad men, in the concrete imagery of what Susanne K. Langer calls *presentational symbols*.[10]

Returning to Lawrence in the context of the opposing creative modes articulated by Nietzsche, one recognizes in his characteristic themes and forms a similar dualism. Simplistic reading tends to attribute to Lawrence a one-sided, exclusively Dionysian sexual ecstasy, primitive religiosity, and intellectual irrationalism. In Lawrence's view, it is true, the times demanded a reassertion of these Dionysian forces to correct the imbalance on the side of Apollonian forces in decadent form—the imbalance on the side of spiritual will, rationalized faith, and sterile reason—which had resulted from the unholy wedlock of the industrial revolution and Christian idealism: the one divorced from natural cycles, the other divorced from religious cycles, and both united in the service of the utilitarian ethic that defined creativity as production, and progress as the proliferation of technology. But Lawrence no more advocated an imbalance on the opposite side than Nietzsche did. In every area of his thought—historiography, theology, psychology, literary criticism—Lawrence makes his plea for a balanced polarity between the Apollonian and the Dionysian; and the effect of much of his fiction derives from the dialectical tension between the two.[11]

In the short novel *The Ladybird* (1923), Lawrence established the theoretical opposition between the Apollonian and the Dionysian in fictional terms. The radical contrast that he sets up rather overtly in this strange story may be useful in illustrating a conflict that is worked out with greater subtlety, complexity, and ambiguity in Lawrence's major fiction. In the novella, the divine and the terrible, in the person of a mysterious stranger, make an incursion into the ordinary life of a young aristocratic British wife as a first step toward reasserting an ancient mythic power as a principle of charismatic leadership to regenerate the war-wasted modern world. If we stand back from the complex surface of the story, in which myths from several different cultures are merged syncretically and the mythic and the actual modulate into each other in an atmosphere of suspended time, what we may see is an abstract design, a Laurentian triad in which two male figures, the one of light, the other of darkness, compete for the soul of modern woman.

Lady Daphne's prototype in Greek mythology is a nymph, the daughter of a river (the Pēnēus or the Ladon) and the beloved of both Apollo and the mortal Leucippus. When Leucippus, disguised as a woman, pursued Daphne, he was discovered and slain by the nymphs. Still pursued by Apollo, who tried to ravish her, Daphne appealed to the goddess Hera, who changed her into the laurel tree, which remained sacred to Apollo. Although the myth is cited in Freudian psychology "as symbolizing a girl's instinctive horror of the sexual act," Robert Graves says that Daphne's name is "a contraction of Daphoene, 'the bloody one,' the goddess in orgiastic mood whose priestesses, the Maenads, chewed laurel leaves as an intoxicant." [12] The modern Lady Daphne, in Lawrence's story, has the same division within herself. From her father's "desperate race" she derives her own wild energy of the blood; from her mother's upbringing she learns "to admire

only the good" (*L,* p. 47). For Lawrence, this conflict
between blood and will would be etiology enough for
almost any malady. Her conscious will determines that
she be gentle and benevolent, "but her blood had
revenge on her." She is associated with death and metaphysical illness: "Her husband was missing in the East.
Her baby had been born dead. Her two darling brothers
were dead. And she was ill, always ill." That her sick-
ness is intended to be generalized as that of the modern
world is evident from Lawrence's statement: "So it is
with strong natures today: shattered from the inside"
(*L,* pp. 46–47). Living on bitter hope, which "had
become almost a curse to her," Daphne anticipates the
apocalypse, almost as if she perceives, though she cannot
articulate it, that the old order must be irrevocably
ended before a new one can emerge: "Why could it not
all be just clean disaster, and have done with it? This
dillydallying with despair was worse than despair"
(*L,* p. 48).

Major Basil Apsley, Lady Daphne's husband, in his
slightly simple-minded humanism, resembles Apollo
not so much as he does Leucippus, his war scar suggesting his symbolic slaying. As a fusion of the two
figures, he represents what has become of the Apollonian impulse in the modern world: in the decline of
its divine and shaping as well as its erotic and heroic
functions, its conscious humanism and commitment
to technology support a war machine. As "a commoner,
son of one of the most famous politicians in England"
(*L,* p. 46),[13] Basil is associated with democratic egalitarian politics, the logical outcome of which, unforeseen
by the respectable older generation of leaders like his
father or Lady Daphne's father, Earl Beveridge, has
been a debasement of culture and the reduction of all
to the lowest common denominator in the hysteria

of war: "the degrading spectacle of the so-called patriots who had been howling their mongrel indecency in the public face. These mongrels had held the Press and the British public in abeyance for almost two years. Their one aim was to degrade and humiliate anything that was proud or dignified remaining in England" (*L,* p. 92). Yet the ordeal of war is, for Basil, a refining process through which he believes that he has arrived at "a higher state of consciousness, and therefore of life. And so, of course, at a higher plane of love. A surprisingly higher plane of love, that you had never suspected the existence of before" (*L,* p. 85). That this "higher plane" is rather lower, in Lawrence's eyes, is made graphically clear as Basil, like the ancient druidic poets of Graves's *The White Goddess* who worship Cynthia or Diana or "la belle dame sans merci," kneels before Daphne in a rapture of courtly love adoration that is really designed to keep her in her place on the pedestal of childlike chastity and out of his marriage bed: ". . . —you perfect child! But that is the beauty of a woman like you: you are so superb and beyond worship, and then such an exquisite naïve child. Who could help worshipping you and loving you: Immortal and mortal together. . . . Ah, darling, you are more goddess than child, you long, limber Isis with sacred hands. White, white, and immortal! . . . I *can't* help kneeling before you, darling. I am no more than a sacrifice to you, an offering. I *wish* I could die in giving myself to you, give you all my blood on your altar, for ever" (*L,* p. 81). Basil's ultimate renunciation of sex in favor of a "pure love" suggests the final abstraction of Apollo, Daphne's would-be ravisher, into pure spirit.

The third member of the triad, Count Johann Dionys Psanek, has no counterpart in the original myth of

Daphne and Apollo but is imported from another to
supplant Apollo as Daphne's pursuer. His name, his
appearance, his language underline his function in the
story to reassert the Dionysian mystery. It is appropriate for Lawrence's figure of male dominance that
his classical prototype, the son of Zeus and the mortal
woman Semele, was called the "twice-born." His mother
was struck by lightning from Zeus and perished, but
Zeus took his son and carried him in his own body
until he was ready for the world.[14] Deriving from two
realms, the mortal and the eternal, Dionysus remained
the god of duality and paradox. He was a god of
fertility, appearing in the spring to awaken the energy
of life, bringing forth the vegetation of the season and
evoking in his followers a divine madness in which they
tore their victims apart and ate their flesh. According
to Walter Otto, in *Dionysus: Myth and Cult,* Dionysus
brought no illusions or fantasies but "the elemental
forms of everything that is creative, everything that is
destructive" so that, in the divine madness he induced,
not only human laws but "even the dimensions of time
and space are no longer valid." [15]

Count Dionys's middle name is, of course, derived
from the god's. His surname, Psanek, he says, means
"outlaw" (*L,* p. 59); it also contains two anagrams,
"asp" and "snake." Dionysus's epiphany at the winter
solstice was as a serpent, and his followers wore serpent-
wreathed crowns.[16] When Lady Daphne was seventeen,
Count Dionys had given her a thimble ringed with a
serpent. The fact that he considers giving up his first
two names and retaining only his last suggests which
part of the Dionysian duality he wants to emphasize
(*L,* pp. 53, 59).

Imagery and symbol associate Count Dionys throughout with the Dionysian nature religion and the rituals

of its annual cycle. One of the major motifs on which
the novella turns is that of death and rebirth. When
Lady Beveridge discovers Count Dionys among the
wounded prisoners in the hospital, the "yellowish
swarthy paste of his flesh" seems drawn "on the face
of one dead," but "his black eyes watched her from that
terrible remoteness of death" (*L,* p. 45). This condition, as much metaphysical as physical, makes him
almost acquiesce in death; but images of life in the
fecund darkness of the earth suggest that, however painful it may be, he will consent to rebirth. When Lady
Daphne visits him in the hospital, he tells her: "No,
no! No, no! If I could be buried deep, very deep down,
where everything is forgotten! But they draw me up,
back to the surface. I would not mind if they buried me
alive, if it were very deep, and dark, and the earth
heavy above" (*L,* p. 53). Dionys calls himself "a subject of the sun" and says, "I belong to the fire-wor-
shippers" (*L,* p. 55). But his is not the bright sun of
Apollo but the dark sun of the underworld: "The true
fire is invisible," he tells Lady Daphne. "Flame, and
the red fire we see burning, has its back to us." It is
here that Lawrence first elaborates the image that was
to become a major symbol in *The Plumed Serpent:*

> Well, then, the yellowness of sunshine—light
> itself—that is only the glancing aside of the real
> original fire. You know that is true. There would be
> no light if there was no refraction, no bits of dust
> and stuff to turn the dark fire into visibility. You
> know that's a fact. And that being so, even the sun is
> dark. It is only his jacket of dust that makes him
> visible. You know that too. And the true sunbeams
> coming towards us flow darkly, a moving darkness of
> the genuine fire. The sun is dark, the sunshine flowing

to us is dark. And light is only the inside-turning
away of the sun's directness that was coming to us.
(*L,* p. 67)

The Apollonian-Dionysian polarity is clear: "The true
living world of fire is dark, throbbing, darker than
blood. Our luminous world that we go by is only the
reverse of this" (*L,* p. 67). Now he tells Lady Daphne,
"The year has turned—the sun must shine at last, even
in England" (*L,* p. 56). Basil and Lady Daphne visit
the Count at Vornich Hall at the winter solstice just
before Christmas (*L,* p. 83), and he visits them at
Thoresway in the spring (*L,* p. 93).

There is an element of Dionysian madness in Count
Dionys. In one of his conversations with Lady Daphne,
he admits to talking absurdly (*L,* p. 54), a suggestion
that his speech derives from his inner perceptions of
reality, not from the logic of the outer world. He tells
her that "the Psaneks have had a ladybird in their
bonnets for many hundred years," a reference to the
family crest, and Lady Daphne replies, "Quite, quite
mad" (*L,* p. 61). Privately she thinks him "An imper-
tinent little fellow! A little madman, really. A little
outsider" (*L,* p. 69), and she determines to keep her
mind on her well-bred husband.

Dionys associates the course of his blood with the
organic cycle of nature, with yellow chestnuts and chat-
tering squirrels, but not with the world of man. Following the Dionysian cycle, he has already made his
northern journey over the North Sea to "the Eskimo in
Siberia, and across the Tundras" where "a white sea-
hawk makes a nest on a high stone": "It is not only a
world of men, Lady Daphne" (*L,* p. 59). The count's
swart, aboriginal appearance (*L,* p. 45) and demonic

visage (*L,* p. 84) link him with the underworld, and the devil in his body (*L,* p. 55) identifies him with Hades. He associates himself with the god of destruction:

". . . I found the God who pulls things down: especially the things that men have put up. Do they not say that life is a search after God, Lady Daphne? I have found my God."

"The god of destruction," she said, blanching.

"Yes—not the devil of destruction, but the god of destruction. The blessed god of destruction. . . . The god of anger, who throws down the steeples and the factory chimneys. Ah, Lady Daphne, he is a man's God. I have found my God, Lady Daphne."
(*L,* p. 73)

With the factories of industrial civilization out of the way, along with the steeples of the traditional Christian faith that supports the established western world order, Dionys can establish a new faith on power rather than on love—or, more accurately, on an elision of power and love, not Christian, submissive love but "profane" love that is elemental and subversive. As if to propose a new creed, he hisses darkly, "his eyes dilated with a ring of fire," an incantation of power: "I believe in the power of my red, dark heart. God has put the hammer in my breast—the little eternal hammer. Hit—hit—hit! It hits on the world of man. It hits, it hits! And it hears the thin sound of cracking. The thin sound of cracking. Hark!" (*L,* p. 74). As Daphne listens, he continues, a strange laugh on his face and a shivering, delicate crackling sound in the air: "You hear it? Yes? Oh, may I live long! May I live long, so that my hammer may strike and strike, and the cracks go

deeper, deeper! Ah, the world of man! Ah, the joy, the
passion in every heart-beat! Strike home, strike true,
strike sure. Strike to destroy it. Strike! Strike! To destroy
the world of man. Ah, God. Ah, God, prisoner of peace.
Do I not know you, Lady Daphne? Do I not? Do I
not?" (*L,* pp. 74–75)

I have quoted this passage at some length because I
want to draw a parallel and a contrast with the incantation of negatives by which Roderick Usher impels the
lady Madeline in Poe's story from the tomb to fall
upon him in an incestuous embrace of death that
fissures the house of Usher so that it literally sinks beneath the surface of the tarn:

> "Now hear it?—yes, I hear it, and *have* heard it.
> Long—long—long—many minutes, many hours,
> many days, have I heard it—yet I dared not—oh, pity
> me, miserable wretch that I am!—I dared not—I
> *dared* not speak! *We have put her living in the
> tomb!* Said I not that my senses were acute? I *now*
> tell you that I heard her feeble first movements in
> the hollow coffin. I heard them—many, many days
> ago—yet I dared not—*I dared not speak!* And
> now—tonight—Ethelred—ha! ha!—the breaking
> of the hermit's door, and the death-cry of the dragon,
> and the clangor of the shield—say, rather, the
> rending of her coffin, and the grating of the iron
> hinges of her prison, and her struggles within the
> coppered archway of the vault! Oh! whither shall
> I fly? Will she not be here anon? Is she not hurrying
> to upbraid me for my haste? Have I not heard her
> footsteps on the stair? Do I not distinguish the heavy
> and horrible beating of her heart? Madman!"—
> here he sprang furiously to his feet, and shrieked
> out his syllables, as if in the effort he were giving

up his soul—"MADMAN! I TELL YOU THAT SHE
NOW STANDS WITHOUT THE DOOR!" [17]

Lawrence's passage in *The Ladybird* employs, without
improving on, Poe's technique of incantatory repetition
and echoes certain of Poe's key words and phrases.
Poe's "long—long—long—" becomes Lawrence's
"hit—hit—hit." Poe's "clangor of the shield" and
"grating of the iron hinges" are replaced by Lawrence's
"thin sound of cracking." The prison of the "coppered
archway" of Madeline's vault becomes the prison of
peace that encompasses Lady Daphne. The incantation
of negatives (the word *not* occurs ten times in Poe's
paragraph) is transmuted into the reiterated image of
striking (the word *hit* occurs six times and the word
strike eight times in the Lawrence passage) and is
echoed in Count Dionys's "Do I not? Do I not?" with
which the passage ends. The frenzied eye of the poet,
the tone of madness in his voice, and the atmosphere
of death that surrounds him are focal elements in both
passages.

Yet in several significant respects, the two passages
are not equivalent. Both their heroes, Roderick Usher
and Count Dionys Psanek, seem literally to incant
their women from their premature burial in the tomb
and to impel them to an embrace of death in an underworld rendezvous. But Usher dominates by sheer will,
Dionys by charismatic power. The distinction is more
than an academic subtlety, for the result is not, ultimately, the same. Lawrence comments in the essay on
Poe in *Studies in Classic American Literature* (1923)
that

the rhythm of American art-activity is dual.
   1. A disintegrating and sloughing of the old
   consciousness.

2. The forming of a new consciousness underneath. (*SCAL*, p. 65)

As an examination of Lawrence's theoretical formulations in historiography, theology, and psychology
shows, this dual rhythm of creation also characterizes
his thinking in other areas. Moreover, Lawrence's
personal emblem, the phoenix, incorporates the same
principle in the cyclic pattern of destruction and re-
synthesis. As he interprets the myth in the third essay
in *The Crown* (1915), the phoenix attains perfection
in wisdom as natural aristocrat, but, rather than main-
taining "her own tight ego," she commits herself to
the flames of experience; thus, she is reduced to the
essential ash from which a new phoenix emerges to
rise toward the same zenith of perfection and to the
same consummation in flame (*C*, p. 382). In *The
Ladybird,* the principle of creative evolution is associated
with the ladybird of the Psanek family crest, which,
Dionys says, "is a descendant of the Egyptian scarabaeus,"
connecting him with the Pharaohs. In a discussion with
Lord and Lady Beveridge, Basil, and Daphne, the
count reveals the scarab to be an emblem of the cycle
of disintegration and renewal:

> "Do you know Fabre?" put in Lord Beveridge.
> "He suggests that the beetle rolling a little ball of
> dung before him, in a dry old field, must have sug-
> gested to the Egyptians the First Principle that set the
> globe rolling. And so the scarab became the symbol
> of the creative principal—or something like that."
> "That the earth is a tiny ball of dry dung is good,"
> said Basil.
> "Between the claws of a ladybird," added Daphne.
> "That is what it is, to go back to one's origin,"
> said Lady Beveridge.

"Perhaps they meant that it was the principle of decomposition which first set the ball rolling," said the Count.

"The ball would have to be *there* first," said Basil.

"Certainly. But it hadn't started to roll. Then the principle of decomposition started it." (*L,* p. 97)

As Lawrence sees it, Poe is concerned with only one side of the duality. Whereas "Fenimore Cooper has the two vibrations going on together," "Poe has only one, only the disintegrative vibration. That makes him more a scientist than an artist" (*SCAL,* p. 65). In terms of the dialectic with which this study is concerned, Lawrence's commitment is to the Dionysian cycle, which follows destruction with a new synthesis. Poe, on the other hand, offers an example of Apollonian rationalism in decadent form, analytic reduction by mechanistic will. He is concerned analytically with psychic processes—or, in Lawrence's words, "with the disintegration-processes of his own psyche"—in tales that are "a concatenation of cause and effect" (*SCAL,* p. 65). Lawrence's is not, then, a hellish vision in the same sense that Poe's is: in Poe the dark forces only destroy, in Lawrence they are ultimately the source of rebirth as well.

To return to *The Ladybird* in this context, Count Dionys, as natural aristocrat, is a spokesman for charismatic power; and Basil, as democratic egalitarian, is a spokesman for Christian love. Dionys is the prophet, if not the agent, of a kind of leadership that Lawrence proposes as a possible means of regeneration for modern Europe, first by finishing the destruction of worn-out cultural traditions already begun in the reductive process of the war, then by resynthesizing civilization around the dynamic center of "the man whose soul is born single, able to be alone, to choose and to command," to whom the masses will turn "Because we see a light in your face, and a burning on your mouth" (*L,* p. 89). To Lawrence's way of thinking, this is not fascism, which he characterizes as bullying by mechanical will, but charismatic leadership of the sort he speaks of in the last chapter of *Movements in European History:*

> A great united Europe of productive working-people, all materially equal, will never be able to continue and remain firm unless it unites also round one great chosen figure, some hero who can lead a great war, as well as administer a wide peace. It all depends on the will of the people. But the will of the people must concentrate in one figure, who is also supreme over the will of the people. He must be chosen, but at the same time responsible to God alone. Here is a problem of which a stormy future will have to evolve a solution. (*MEH,* p. 344)

Those who have lived through the "stormy future" that Lawrence foresaw are likely to find his leadership proposition rather less promising than he did. Lady Daphne, who has a feminist side, perceives immediately that, in a system where men cannot criticize their chosen leader, women will no longer be able to criticize their husbands (*L,* p. 90). Significantly, it is Major Basil Apsley who recognizes that "there is really an allowable distinction between responsible power and bullying" and that Count Dionys means the former (*L,* p. 91).

Count Dionys speaks for a quasi-religious relationship between the Dionysian leader and his followers. Lady Daphne's Apollonian consciousness, on the other hand, seems "to make a great gulf between her and the lower classes, the unconscious classes. . . . She could never meet in real contact anyone but a super-conscious, finished being like herself: or like her husband" (*L,* p. 99). As Lawrence's representative of the British upper class, then, she must make her journey of initiation into the unconscious with Count Dionys as her guide. Unlike Roderick Usher, who impels the lady Madeline from the tomb by a litany of negatives, Dionys, "half-unconscious," calls Daphne to his room by crooning "in a small, high-pitched, squeezed voice. . . . a curious noise: the sound of a man who is alone in his own blood: almost the sound of a man who is going to be executed" (*L,* p. 99). The song Dionys sings in his native dialect is of "a woman who was a swan, and who loved a hunter by the marsh. So she became a woman and married and had three children. Then in the night one night the king of the swans called to her to come back, or else he would die. So slowly she turned into a swan again, and slowly she opened her wide, wide wings, and left her husband and her children" (*L,* p. 102). This Dionysian parable—which has affinities with ballads, such as "The Great Silkie of Sule Skerry" (Child, no. 113), as well as fairy tales, such as "Beauty and the Beast"—serves to associate Count Dionys with the principle of divine destruction by comparing him to the swan, which Lawrence identifies in *The Crown* as "one of the symbols of divine corruption with its reptile feet buried in the ooze and mud, its voluptuous form yielding and embracing the ooze of water, its beauty white and cold and terrifying, like the dead beauty of the moon, like the water-lily, the sacred lotus, its neck and head like the snake, it is for us a flame of the cold white fire of flux, the phosphorescence of cor-

ruption, the salt, cold burning of the sea which corrodes
all it touches, coldly reduces every sun-built form to
ash, to the original elements" (C, p. 403).

In interpreting the significance of the sexual consummation between Daphne and Dionys, it is well to
bear in mind Lawrence's statement in *The Crown* that
"when a man seeks a woman, he seeks not a consummation in union, but a frictional reduction" (C, p. 394).
The reduction, however, should be followed by rebirth.
The image of the dark sun, which is associated with
the scarab symbolism of the Psanek family crest, is
reinforced in the scene in which Lady Daphne visits
the count's room. When her fingertips merely touch
his arm, "a flame went over him that left him no more
a man" but the figure of a deity: "He was something
seated in flame, in flame unconscious, seated erect, like
an Egyptian King-god in the statues" (L, p. 103). The
allusion is possibly to Khepri, who was identified with
the rising sun and thus with the eternal renewal of
life.[18] Lady Daphne kneels involuntarily and presses her
face and hands against his feet and ankles. The words of
the song also associate Dionys with Zeus, "the king of
the swans." Where Daphne is concerned, one may ask
with Yeats,

> Did she put on his knowledge with his power
> Before the indifferent beak could let her drop?
> ("Leda and the Swan," lines 14–15)

Count Dionys's knowledge is what Lawrence calls
"blood consciousness," the ancient, dark, mysterious
power that Lawrence reasserts, not as the sole value but
as a corrective to the imbalance on the side of the
modern, light, rational "mental consciousness." As
Lawrence says in his essay "Nathaniel Hawthorne and

The Scarlet Letter" in *Studies in Classic American Literature:*

> Blood-consciousness overwhelms, obliterates, and annuls mind-consciousness.
> Mind-consciousness extinguishes blood-consciousness, and consumes the blood.
> We are all of us conscious in both ways. And the two ways are antagonistic in us.
> They will always remain so.
> That is our cross. (*SCAL,* p. 85)

There is a sense in which the mind-conscious Lady Daphne does "put on his knowledge with his power." Like such Laurentian heroines as Kate Leslie in *The Plumed Serpent* and Connie in *Lady Chatterley's Lover,* she is regenerated sexually and integrated psychologically by her contact with the destructive power of the blood-conscious male: "She was so still, like a virgin girl. And it was this quiet, intact quality of virginity in her which puzzled [her husband] most" (*L,* p. 105), so that Basil renounces sexual relations with her in preference for a "pure love" reminiscent of medieval Mariolatry.

Count Dionys, employing an ancient metaphorical link between sexual orgasm and death, says to Daphne:

> Now you are mine. In the dark you are mine. And when you die you are mine. . . . In the night, in the dark, and in death, you are mine. And that is for ever. No matter if I must leave you. I shall come again from time to time. In the dark you are mine. But in the day I cannot claim you. I have no power in the day, and no place. So remember. When darkness comes, i shall always be in the darkness of

you. . . . So don't forget—you are the night wife of
the ladybird, while you live and even when you
die. (*L,* p. 104)

The metaphysical pun turns on the principle of reduction shared by both death and sex. As Lawrence puts
it in *The Crown,* "In sex, we have plunged the quick
of creation deep into the cold flux of reduction, corruption, till the quick is extinguished" (*C,* p. 401). Picking
up the swan image, he elaborates: "When the swan
first rose out of the marshes, it was a glory of creation.
But when we turn back, to seek its consummation again,
it is a fearful flower of corruption" (*C,* p. 403). The
narrative song Dionys sings suggests just such a turning
back.

The principle that Henry Miller calls "creative
death" has long been recognized as a central Laurentian
concept. One critic, Colin Clarke, in *River of Dissolution: D. H. Lawrence and English Romanticism,* has
explored extensively the implications of Lawrence's
related concepts of destruction, dissolution, decomposition, corruption, and reduction, concepts with which
not all Lawrence scholars are comfortable.[19] My purpose
in introducing these ideas here is to identify the "destructive element," to borrow Stein's phrase in Conrad's
Lord Jim, as a living element in which Lawrence's
most vital characters must, as Stein advises, immerse
themselves. As Clarke correctly perceives, "What is
most in question . . . is the distinction between corruption that is creative and corruption that is not." [20]
Lawrence himself provides a partial answer to the
question in *The Crown* in a passage cited briefly by
Clarke: "And corruption, like growth, is only divine
when it is pure, when all is given up to it. If it be experienced as a controlled activity within an intact whole,

this is vile. . . . When corruption goes on within the living womb, this is unthinkable" (*C,* p. 403). It has seemed to some critics that Clarke blurs the distinction between the two forms of corruption, the one leading to life, the other to death,[21] in such passages as the following:

> I have emphasized throughout this book that in Lawrence's best work the negative potentialities in dissolution are apt to be held in tension with the positive. . . . For degradation is not . . . a process that Birkin and Ursula altogether emerge from, renewed. Something like this is intimated at one level, certainly; but what is more pervasively suggested is that the two processes—renewal and dissolution, regeneration and the descent into corruption —can never in fact be dissociated; or more accurately, that there is after all only the one process, the ambivalent process of reduction. Accordingly, we find that every intimation that Birkin and Ursula are liberated, or "re-born," is undercut or obscurely qualified.[22]

As a statement about complexity of character in Lawrence's major works of fiction, this is a tenable view. Clarke rightly emphasizes an ambivalence of character even in "creative death," a tension arising out of the characters' struggles to make viable moral choices in a world characterized by moral ambiguity and flux. Their struggles are necessarily made without the certitude of those who accept the status quo, and the results to which their choices lead are not unmixed.

In the theories that underlie his fictional practice, Lawrence presents the two sides of the dialectical tension in terms of a radical contrast and asserts that morality consists in establishing a balance in tension between the two. In the discussion that follows the passage Clarke cites from *The Crown,* Lawrence draws a clear distinction between the two forms of corruption, forms that, in the context of the present discussion, may be designated the Apollonian and the Dionysian. To the Apollonian consciousness, corruption is an analytic or sensational function of a linear process under the control of the ego. To the Dionysian consciousness, corruption is a spontaneous function of a cyclic process in the creative unconscious. Lawrence declares:

> We cannot subject a divine process to a static will, not without blasphemy and loathsomeness. The static will must be subject to the process of reduction, also. For the pure absolute, the Holy Ghost, lies also in the relationship which is made manifest by the departure *ad infinitum,* of the opposing elements.
>
> Corruption will at last break down for us the deadened forms, and release us into the infinity. But the static ego, with its will-to-persist, neutralizes both life and death, and utterly defies the Holy Ghost. (*C*, pp. 403–404)

Creative destruction is, of course, a vital process of nature. Moreover, the reductive activities of modern society—war, the disintegration of cultural institutions, the dissolution of older moral traditions, the fragmentation of society, and the compartmentalization of the individual—affect everyone simply because everyone is in the society. So the question is not whether to participate in destruction but in what spirit to do so. On the one hand, one may keep intact one's egoistic will as a static entity within which one seeks the sensation of reduction, whether in parlor games of analysis or in bedroom games of sexual manipulation and experimentation. On the other hand, one may submit one's whole self, including one's static will and one's "tight ego," to the whole cycle of destruction and regeneration: "We may give ourselves utterly to destruction. Then our conscious forms are destroyed along with us, and something new must arise. But we may not have corruption within ourselves as sensationalism, our skin and outer form intact. To destroy life for the preserving of a static, rigid and outer shell, a glassy envelope, this is the lugubrious activity of the men who fight to save democracy and to end all fighting" (C, p. 404). Lawrence does not want to end all fighting, because that would mean that one side of the duality had finally won. Quoting the lines

> *The Lion and the Unicorn*
> *Were fighting for the Crown,*

Lawrence says, "Thus we portray ourselves in the field of the royal arms. The whole history is the fight, the whole *raison d'être.*" "This is a terrible position," he admits, "to have for a *raison d'être* a purpose which, if once fulfilled, would of necessity entail the cessation from existence of both opponents. They would both cease to be, if either of them really won in the fight which is their sole reason for existing" (C, pp. 365–366). They are not fighting *for* the crown; they are fighting *beneath* it, he tells us, and the crown is "upon their fight." Lawrence does not, in this contest, favor the Dionysian lion any more than he does the Apollonian unicorn. He speaks, rather, for a balanced opposition between the two, with the crown, here a figure for the Holy Ghost, as a principle of unity in opposition.

Notes

1. Henry Miller, *The Wisdom of the Heart* (Norfolk, Conn.: New Directions Books, 1941), p. 5. See also Wallace G. Kay, "The Cortege of Dionysus: Lawrence and Giono," *Southern Quarterly* 4 (1966): 159–171, and "Dionysus, D. H. Lawrence, and Jean Giono: Further Considerations," *Southern Quarterly* 6 (1968): 394–414.

2. Friedrich Nietzsche, *Die Geburt Der Tragödie,* in *Werke,* I, 19, as quoted in Joseph Campbell, *The Masks of God: Creative Mythology* (New York: Viking Press, 1968), p. 334.

3. Ibid.

4. Campbell, *Masks of God,* pp. 333–334.

5. Ibid., p. 352.

6. Ibid., p. 353. See Rudolf Otto, *The Idea of the Holy* (London, New York, Toronto: Geoffrey Cumberlege, Oxford University Press, 1946), pp. 5–7.

7. Nietzsche, *Die Geburt Der Tragödie,* as quoted in Campbell, *Masks of God,* pp. 337–338.

8. Walter Kaufmann, *Nietzsche: Philosopher, Psychologist, Antichrist* (Cleveland and New York: World Publishing Co., 1966), pp. 108–109.

9. Ibid., p. 109.

10. Susanne K. Langer, *Philosophy in a New Key* (New York: New American Library, Mentor Book Edition, 1956), p. 236.

11. D. H. Lawrence's works are cited parenthetically in my text by abbreviated title and page numbers as follows:

C: *The Crown,* in *Phoenix II: Uncollected, Unpublished, and Other Prose Works by D. H. Lawrence,* ed. Warren Roberts and Harry T. Moore (New York: Viking Press, 1968).

L: *The Ladybird,* in *Four Short Novels by D. H. Lawrence* (New York: Viking Press, Compass Books, 1965).

MEH: *Movements in European History* (Oxford: Oxford University Press, Humphrey Milford, 1925).

SCAL: Studies in Classic American Literature (New York: Viking Press, Compass Books, 1966).

12. Sir Paul Harvey, ed., *The Oxford Companion to Classical Literature* (Oxford: Oxford University Press, 1955), p. 131, and Robert Graves, *The Greek Myths,* 2 vols. (New York: George Braziller, 1959), p. 18.

13. On one level, *The Ladybird* is a *roman à clef* in which Lady Cynthia Asquith figures as Lady Daphne; her husband, the Honorable Herbert Asquith, son of Herbert Henry Asquith (the prime minister from 1908 to 1916) and who saw active service in France and Flanders (1914–1918), figures as Major Basil Apsley; and Lawrence himself is imaginatively portrayed as Count Dionys.

14. Walter F. Otto, *Dionysus: Myth and Cult,* trans. Robert B. Palmer (Bloomington and London: Indiana University Press, 1965), p. 65.

15. Ibid., pp. 95–96.

16. Ibid. See, especially, plate 6, opposite p. 94, depicting a maenad in serpent-wreathed crown.

17. Edgar Allan Poe, "The Fall of the House of Usher," in *The Literature of the United States,* ed. Walter Blair, Theodore Hornberger, Randall Stewart, and James E. Miller, Jr., 2 vols., 3rd ed. (Glenview, Ill., and London: Scott, Foresman and Co., 1971), I, 782.

18. Georges Posener, *A Dictionary of Egyptian Civilization,* trans. Alix Macfarlane (London: Methuen and Co., 1962), p. 252.

19. See, e.g., Mark Spilka, "Lawrence Up-tight, or the Anal Phase Once Over," *Novel* 4 (Spring 1971): 252–267, and the replies by George Ford, Frank Kermode, and Colin Clarke, *Novel* 5 (Fall 1971): 54–70.

20. Colin Clarke, *River of Dissolution: D. H. Lawrence and English Romanticism* (New York: Barnes and Noble, 1969), p. 70.

21. Charles Rossman, for example, states this view in "Four Versions of D. H. Lawrence," *The D. H. Lawrence Review* 6 (Spring 1973): 55.

22. Clarke, *River of Dissolution,* p. 129.

FIVE

Stephen Dedalus and the Spiritual-Heroic Refrigerating Apparatus: Art and Life in Joyce's *Portrait*

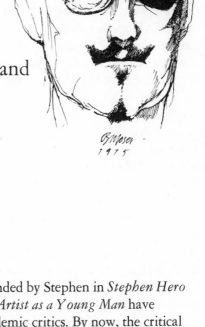

Charles Rossman

THE aesthetics expounded by Stephen in *Stephen Hero* and *A Portrait of the Artist as a Young Man* have always fascinated academic critics. By now, the critical shadow cast by the aesthetics has grown very long, indeed. But for all the erudite words about Aquinas stasis, and kinesis, about *integritas, consonantia, claritas,* and *quidditas,* critics frequently skirt Joyce's real subject, which gives the aesthetics their meaning: a young man's painful, perhaps doomed, effort to define and liberate the self. Criticism tends to regard the detached aesthe-

tics as a self-contained entity and to ignore the inter-
pretive context provided by the rest of the novel. As a
result, little has been said about the manner in which
the aesthetics express Stephen's character and experiences, or the way that many of Stephen's personal
problems find resolution or perpetuation in aesthetic
experience. Everyone agrees that Stephen's discourse
on Shakespeare in *Ulysses* reveals more about Stephen
than Hamlet; yet that the same is true of Stephen's
aesthetics in the earlier novels has gone relatively
unappreciated.

However, recent work by three persuasive critics—
Hugh Kenner, S. L. Goldberg, and Robert Scholes—
carries discussion of the aesthetics into a wider arena.
Because their work has generated my own, I can best
begin with a brief account of their ideas.

Kenner and Goldberg make the theory of the epiphany, included in *Stephen Hero* but omitted from
Portrait, crucial to our understanding of both books and
Ulysses as well. Both Kenner and Goldberg consider
the concept of the epiphany an integral and permanent
part of Joyce's own aesthetics, and both therefore regard
its absence from *Portrait* as an ironic undercutting of
Stephen Dedalus. According to Kenner, Joyce composed *Portrait* with "his eye constantly on the epic
sequel," *Ulysses,* and the ironic deflation of Stephen it
would accomplish.[1] Thus, to set Stephen up for his fall,
Joyce makes him expound a Neoplatonic aesthetics
that Stephen naively believes to be Aristotelean and
Thomist. The aesthetics are weakened because, in
Kenner's words, "the crucial principle of epiphanization
has been withdrawn" (p. 121). Goldberg interprets
the epiphany as essentially a quality of emotional and
perceptual stasis that enables detached observation.[2]
Its absence from *Portrait,* in Goldberg's view, opens a

rift between art and life and leads Stephen toward a
Neoplatonic idealism. Kenner and Goldberg agree,
then, in finding the Stephen of *Stephen Hero* more
realistic, the Stephen of *Portrait* more idealistic. Scholes
takes issue specifically with Kenner and Goldberg and
exactly reverses their judgments. Scholes finds Stephen
"more of an idealist in *Stephen Hero* and more of a
realist in *Portrait*." [3] Far too much has been made of the
importance of the epiphany in Joyce's works, Scholes
believes. The whole notion of the epiphany, as Scholes
sees it, reflects a "Platonic idealism" that both Joyce and
Stephen outgrew following the composition of *Stephen
Hero*. It is a heady term and smug concept, implying
by definition the separation of the observer from the
world and assuming his superiority to his environment.
Scholes thus interprets the omission of the epiphany
from *Portrait* as a sign of Stephen's and Joyce's maturity
and of Stephen's engagement with the concrete par-
ticulars of experience.

The question at the heart of this controversy—
whether Stephen in a given book is more a "realist"
or an "idealist"—is fundamental. Asking it, we confront
not only basic questions about Stephen's character and
Joyce's tone, but also three less apparent yet equally
crucial questions: (1) What is the nature of Stephen's
experience of the phenomenal world of external "reality"? (2) What is the source of the iconography and
thematic content of Stephen's art? And, consequently,
(3) What is the relationship of life, art, and Stephen-
as-creator? It is these questions that I will deal with
in the rest of this essay. Because Kenner, Goldberg, and
Scholes all imply that Stephen in *Stephen Hero* somehow speaks for Joyce but disagree sharply about the
substance of those statements, I turn first to a comparison of Stephen's aesthetics in *Stephen Hero* with those

of the youthful Joyce, as a preliminary to comparison
of *Stephen Hero* with *Portrait.*

Robert Scholes's assertion that Stephen's aesthetics
in *Stephen Hero* are Neoplatonic makes him only the
most recent and authoritative of a long line of critics
who have found either Joyce's or Stephen's aesthetics in
some one of their versions, "idealist," "Neoplatonic,"
or "romantic." It is important to emphasize, then, that
regardless of what we conclude about *Stephen,* Joyce
himself had little in common, either temperamentally
or philosophically, with AE in *Ulysses,* who affirms
that "art has to reveal to us ideas, formless spiritual
essences," or with Buck Mulligan, who asserts that
"any object, intensely regarded, may be a gate of access
to the incorruptible eon of the gods." On the contrary,
a plethora of direct statements from Joyce justifies the
following as descriptions of the convictions he formed
as a young man and that, I believe, suffused his artistic
theories and creations throughout his life:

1. The basic fact of human existence is that being
   is *in* and *of* this world.
2. Human identity is a temporal flux, usefully
   understood in terms of Aristotle's conceptions
   of potentiality and entelechy. Human growth is
   the actualization of potential through acts of will
   implementing conscious choice (Aristotle's
   praxis).
3. "Reality" consists of objective, public facts that
   are, nevertheless, subject to distortions of perception and understanding bred by subjective states.
4. "Truth" is a relationship between perceiver and
   object that lets the object be seen for what it is,
   lets the thing speak for itself, free from the per-

ceptual coloring of fear, disgust, desire, or similar emotions and moods (akin to the reposeful, yet active contemplation or beholding that Aristotle called *theoria*).

Joyce's first statement that suggests these conclusions is his essay "Drama and Life," written at age eighteen. In it, Joyce scorns the "mistaken insistence" on the "religious," "moral," "beautiful," and "idealizing tendencies" of art. He argues for "life—real life" as the proper subject of drama, boldly proclaiming: "We must accept [life] as we see it before our eyes, men and women as we meet them in the real world, not as we apprehend them in the world of faery. The great human comedy in which each has share, gives limitless scope to the true artist." [4] Two years later, in "James Clarence Mangen," Joyce admonishes the "impatient temper" of romanticism that sees "no fit abode here for its ideals" and so turns to "insensible figures." The romantic errs, Joyce says, in showing no patience for "any method which bends upon these present things and so works upon them and fashions them that the quick intelligence may go beyond them to their meaning, which is still unuttered" (*CW,* p. 74).

In "Drama and Life," Joyce warned that aestheticism too easily becomes "anaemic spirituality," and stressed "truth," rather than beauty, as the "real domain of art." Three years later in the "Paris Notebook," truth gives way to beauty: "The apprehension of the beautiful [is] the end of all art," he writes (*CW,* p. 144). But this reversal in no way indicates a surge of aestheticism of the anaemically spiritual sort. Joyce consistently roots his speculations in the concrete and the tangible. To his praise of beauty, for instance, he carefully adds that "beauty is a quality of something seen." And throughout both the "Paris Notebook" and the "Pola Notebook," containing Joyce's speculations on art, which he worked out for himself during 1903–1904, words like *sensible, matter, object,* and *sensible object* recur. Finally, in a letter written two years later, Joyce reaffirms the artistic imperative to deal with the concrete facts of experience: "I have written *Dubliners* . . . with the conviction that he is a very bold man who dares to alter in the presentment, still more to deform, whatever he has seen and heard." [5]

These remarks, drawn from a six-year period, reveal Joyce's un-Platonic commitment to the actual world of tangible fact. Joyce's personal aesthetics eschewed idealism, Neoplatonism, romanticism, and other methods that deal with the "world of faery" and "insensible figures"—AE's "spiritual essences." Far from displaying a supercilious disregard for his environment, as Scholes implies about both Joyce and the first version of Stephen, Joyce consciously advocated the undistorted presentation of "these present things."

Yet Joyce at twenty-four was no naturalist documenting sense data with a cameralike fidelity, confident that appearances equal reality. In fact, Joyce was acutely aware of the frequent deceptiveness of appearances and of the reality of physical change, as Plato himself had been. And he made his metaphysical doubts about the authenticity of appearances part of his earliest aesthetic principles. The same essays quoted above indicate his belief that literature must go beyond the mere recording of fact to reveal the meaning in the facts and the universal in the concrete. Here lies, I believe, the source of the mistaken conclusion that Joyce was a symbolist in the manner of Baudelaire or the early Yeats or AE as portrayed in *Ulysses.* Yet neither Joyce nor Stephen in *Stephen Hero,* despite Robert Scholes's remarks to the contrary, evinces a belief in timeless, divine essences, in the sense of pure forms or of ideals antecedent to the concrete phenomena that reflect them, according to the mystical formula "as above, so below." Phenomena, for Joyce, do not reflect transcendent realities existing on some other plane. Rather, the meaning of phenomena resides *within,* intricately bound up with the sensible object that is its form. Similarly, the universals Joyce seeks are experiential and inferential, more like the "laws" of science, or the inductions of Aristotle from "sensible spatial magnitudes," [6] than the ideals of Plato. "Drama and Life" makes this explicit: "Human society is the embodiment of changeless laws which the whimsicalities and circumstances of men and women involve and overwrap. . . . Drama has to do with the underlying laws first . . . and only secondarily with the motley agents who bear them out. . . . By drama I understand the interplay of passions to portray truth. . . . If a play or a work of music or a picture presents the everlasting hopes, desires and hates of us, or deals with a symbolic presentment of our widely related nature, albeit a phase of that nature, then it is drama" (*CW,* pp. 40–41). One hears the echo of Aristotle here, in the subordination of character to action, and I suspect Aristotle's pervasive influence in all of Joyce's contemporaneous speculations on truth, beauty, spiritual activities, and the relation of the concrete to universals. While art, for Joyce, clearly seeks to lay bare the meaning of perceived things, it maintains an Aristotelean commitment to the earth as a "fit abode . . . for its ideals." Joyce strove in his art to bridge the gap between appearance and reality, and the concrete and universal. In this effort, he consciously rejected Neoplatonic dualism and evolved a series of methods for entering *into* phenomena: the epiphany,

symbolism, his later use of the myths of Daedalus
and Ulysses, his artistic application of Vico's ideas, and
ultimately the circularity of *Finnegans Wake*.

Stephen in *Stephen Hero* shares his creator's earnest
involvement with the tangible world. An early scene
illustrates: "After breakfast he took the tram for town,
settling himself on the front seat outside with his face
to the wind. He got down off the tram at Amiens St
Station instead of going on to the Pillar because he
wished to partake in the morning life of the city. This
morning walk was pleasant for him and there was no
face that passed him on its way to its commercial
prison but he strove to pierce to the motive centre of
its ugliness. . . . As he walked thus through the ways of
the city he had his ears and eyes ever prompt to receive
impressions." [7] This episode demonstrates that Stephen,
as Robert Scholes says, feels himself superior to his
environment. But Stephen's "superiority" is not the
world-weary scorn of the tangible and the distrust of
the emotions and senses that are essential to Neoplatonism. It is merely the smug confidence in one's own
greater intelligence, sensitivity, and beauty commonly
found among gifted adolescents. Stephen is exuberantly
part of the world, at home in it even when it frustrates
and angers him, as we see from the pains he takes to
indulge his senses—riding atop the tram to feel the
wind against his face and getting down before his
destination, "ever prompt to receive impressions."

The scene also reveals Stephen's keen desire to move
past the mere experience of sights and sounds to their
interpretation, "to pierce to the motive centre." Stephen,
refusing like Joyce to accept appearance as the whole
of reality, conceives of phenomena as penetrable appearances with an intelligible core that he might grasp. He
is characteristically found brooding over the gestures,

words, silences, and deeds of friends, enemies, relatives, and priests, trying to puzzle out their meanings. The image of penetration to a significant center frequently depicts this effort. Concerning Emma, for example, Stephen suspects a "point of illwill" residing "in the centre of her amiableness" (*SH*, p. 68). And Joyce employs the image in a noteworthy early passage that describes Stephen's speculations about the nature of art as a specific instance of his general quest to interpret everything that he perceives: "Stephen did not attach himself to art in any spirit of youthful dilettantism but strove to pierce to the significant heart of everything" (*SH*, p. 33).

Just as Stephen's impulse to understand art is expressive of his character and continuous with his other activities, so too are the conclusions that he reaches, the aesthetic principles themselves. His aesthetics, like Joyce's, insist that art draw forth and reveal the meaning inherent in the sensible world. Early in the book, for example, Stephen writes his essay "Art and Life," which is too often ignored by critics eager to focus on the much later passages dealing with the epiphany. In "Art and Life," Stephen defines the artist as a man "gifted with twin faculties, a selective faculty and a reproductive faculty." The "selective faculty" enables the artist to "disentangle the subtle soul of the image from its mesh of defining circumstances" (*SH*, pp. 77–78). "Soul" here clearly signifies some *indwelling* essence or meaning, not readily perceivable, that serves as the experiential source of art. "Art and Life" goes on to explain and elaborate the relationship of experience to art. "A classical style," Stephen says, "is the only legitimate process from one world [experience] to another [art]." Stephen then offers a definition of the classical temper borrowed from Joyce's own essay

"James Clarence Mangen." He contrasts classicism first with mere realism, which concerns itself with the "portrayal of externals . . . the manners and customs of societies," then with the "spiritual anarchy" of the unsatisfied romantic temper, which turns impatiently away from the concrete world of experience to portray "insensible figures" without "solid bodies." The true poet, possessed of the "selective" and "reproductive" faculties, avoids both extremes—the reductive material-ism of the realist and the disembodied spirituality of the romantic; "[he] chooses rather to bend upon these present things and so to work upon them and fashion them that the quick intelligence may go beyond them to their meaning which is still unuttered."

The aesthetics of "Art and Life," then, parallel Joyce's own in explicitly rejecting the ancient tradition of Platonic idealism, which views, in Robert Scholes's words, "the actual thing [as] merely a symbol of some ideal thing." [8] And if we turn to the passages defining the epiphany with the concepts from "Art and Life" in mind, it is clear that the "selective faculty" and the "classical temper" provide the conceptual germ for the notion of the epiphany. Stephen defines the epiphany as "a sudden spiritual manifestation" that occurs during "the most delicate and evanescent of moments" (*SH*, p. 211). The epiphany is "the gropings of a spiritual eye which seeks to adjust its vision to an exact focus." But his words do not illustrate what Scholes calls Stephen's "neo-Platonic insistence on spiritual manifes-tations." They merely elaborate his earlier description of the artist's "selective faculty." Neither do Stephen's words imply the separation of the observer and the world that Scholes attributes to them. Rather, Stephen carefully divides his emphasis between perceiver and external object, and he assumes a potential harmony between them. He intends to define the delicately balanced relationship between the subjective intelligence and the external world that allows objects to reveal their meanings to the receptive observer. The spiritual eye gropes outward to apprehend meanings "out there" in the world, in such objects of sense experience as a Ballast Office clock. To render this externality, Stephen speaks of the "subtle soul" of things and insists that in epiphany it is the *object* that achieves epiphany: "Its soul, its whatness, leaps to us from the vestment of its appearance" (*SH,* p. 213).

It should be unequivocal by this point that whatever else Joyce and Stephen outgrew between the composition of *Stephen Hero* and *Portrait,* it was not an idealistic temperament. Neither Joyce nor Stephen accepts, in art or life, a metaphysical dualism that postulates two worlds, one physical and one ideal. And neither shows any sympathy for the other dichotomies that Neoplatonism tends toward—such as a dissociation of mind and body or a radical divorcement of art from the experienced world. In *Stephen Hero,* artist, art, and the phenomenal world all stand in intimate relationship. I here offer, as final evidence in support of my conclusions, the testimony of two of Stephen's acquaintances. First, his friend Lynch, who puts in starkly physical terms the intimacy of art with the facts of life: "Stephen's estheticism united with a sane and conscienceless acceptance of the animal needs of a young man" (*SH,* p. 151). Second, Father Artifoni, the Italian priest who concludes that Stephen was "a young man who could not conceive a divorce between art and nature" (*SH,* pp. 170–171). No matter how ethereal Stephen's speculations about truth and beauty become, he maintains his root tie to the physical world. "Life is now—this is life," Stephen tells Cranly: "To walk nobly on the surface of the earth" (*SH*, p. 142).

On June 16, 1904, James Joyce—at twenty-two already the author of numerous essays and poems, a play, some short fiction, and part of a novel—fell in love with Nora Barnacle. Within a few months, they were living together unmarried on the continent, and Nora was pregnant. Comparison of Joyce's circumstances with those of Stephen Dedalus is instructive. Like Joyce, Stephen was a twenty-two–year–old aspiring author on June 16, 1904, in the book Joyce wrote to memorialize the day, *Ulysses.* Yet Stephen, if for the moment we regard *Portrait* and *Ulysses* as a single personal history, has written pitifully little. And, far from falling in love on that date, Stephen visits a whorehouse, where he plays the piano and dances a bit, smashes a lamp in a cathartic moment, and leaves without availing himself of the erotic pleasures of the establishment. At the close of *Portrait,* Stephen had gone exuberantly forward to his voluntary exile in Paris, calling "Welcome O life!" But *Ulysses,* the portrait of Stephen *after* his lyric flight from the squalor of the Dublin labyrinth, emphatically reveals the pathetic gap between Stephen's intentions and his achievements, between his potential and his stunted artistic growth. On June 16, 1904, the sought-after "reality of experience" is actualized as embittered self-contempt, gnawing guilt, a pained sense of failed mission, and renewed, directionless wandering within the humiliating Irish labyrinth.

Why has Stephen in *Ulysses* not fulfilled the potential he showed in *Portrait?* Glancing backward with the advantage of hindsight, some readers have concluded that Stephen was never a potential artist at all, never more than a mere posturing aesthete, whose pretensions are exposed in *Portrait* by Joyce's irony and in *Ulysses* by the simple brutal facts. But this extreme view vastly overstates the effects of Joyce's irony and, consequently, seriously distorts Stephen's character and Joyce's attitude toward his brash young hero. For, in fact, the triumphant mood at the close of *Portrait* and the embittered reality of failure in *Ulysses* both depend on Stephen's *authentic potential* as an artist. Therein lies Joyce's point. He has not merely indulged the sport of deflating a pompous, somewhat priggish aesthete, the way some critics would have us believe.[9] Joyce has drawn a portrait of a soul-imprisoning labyrinth, whose walls were far higher than Stephen Dedalus knew. Stephen does not learn how deeply embedded and far-reaching are the corrosive effects of his Dublin environment until very late in *Ulysses,* when he taps his brow and acknowledges, "in here it is I must kill the priest and king." [10]

As Hugh Kenner says, "One cannot escape one's Dublin." [11] Or as Joyce himself put it, Stephen has a shape that cannot be changed. Stephen's physical departure from Ireland is not a liberating flight past the nets of family, church, and country. Beneath the brave appearance of Daedalian flight persist old patterns of behavior that guarantee Stephen's defeat. It is a running *from,* but not a running *to*—reactive flight from the environment that has formed and constrained him, but *not* conscious affirmation of a specific, preferable alternative. Neither is his flight a self-aware transformation of the introjected and internalized "Dublin," of the imprint on Stephen's soul made by the hateful nets of the outer world. Stephen has not yet learned that the nets that entangle him are within. Consequently, his triumphant cry of "Welcome, O life" has no content in terms of future behavior, but merely expresses his self-deceived exhilaration.

In revising *Stephen Hero* into the published version of *Portrait,* Joyce made two changes in Stephen's character that lead him inevitably to a voluntary exile, at the book's end, whose premises can only perpetuate the containment of Stephen's potential. First, in sharp contrast with the "sane and conscienceless acceptance of the animal needs of a young man" exhibited in *Stephen Hero,* Stephen in *Portrait* is deeply alienated from his own physicality. He swings pendulumlike from fits of shame and even hatred of his own sexuality, to furtive, guilty satisfaction of blind rut with prostitutes. His book-long effort to repudiate his body never frees him from his "animal needs"; it only cripples him and drains his energy, fragmenting the integrity of his being and forcing body and soul into separate compartments. The second distinct change in Stephen's character is a corollary to his denial of the flesh: Stephen is also alienated from *external* reality. Whereas the first Stephen persistently aims in both art and life to discover the meaning of external reality, Stephen in *Portrait* rarely engages the world-as-it-is and instead fluctuates between distorted perception of the outer world, weary scorn of it, and open flight from it. Stephen in *Stephen Hero* thrives in the world, Stephen in *Portrait* feels himself a victimized prisoner in the world. In short, the later Stephen frequently deserves the descriptive term so often misapplied to his prototype in *Stephen Hero:* Neoplatonic idealist.

Stephen begins to acquire a distorted image of reality with the novel's first lines, when his father offers him a sentimentalized version of the past: "Once upon a Thereafter, family and church expurgate the child's time *and a very good time it was*" (italics added).

reality in numerous subtle ways—by preventing him from playing with the Protestant girl Eileen, by ruling out some expressions as too bad to use and some boys as too rough to play with, and by teaching him "never to peach on a fellow." Stephen learns fast and soon conjures up for himself ideals with which to measure the perceived world and find it wanting. His mother, for example, is "not so nice" when she cries. His father, he imagines, will soon be "higher than a magistrate." He anticipates a "lovely" journey home from Clongowes for the Christmas holiday, on a "chocolate train with cream facings," and his arrival at a cheery, harmonious, ivy-covered home. He doubts that a priest could be genuinely angry or cruel, because "a priest would know what a sin is and not do it." [12] Reality, of course, stands in shabby and painfully disappointing contrast to his dreams.

Almost from the beginning, Stephen simply blots out painful or disappointing realities and turns his attention inward. Thus, he pretends not to see his mother when she approaches tears, and he closes the flaps of his ears to shut out the sounds of the refectory. An especially significant example of this turning inward occurs when Stephen loses to Jack Lawton in heated classroom competition. Flushed with excitement and confusion, Stephen suddenly isolates himself from events in the classroom and withdraws into his imagination. His face grows cool as he contemplates beautiful colors and the ideal image of a green rose. In the novel's opening scene, Stephen had retreated from a painful reality by hiding underneath a table. In the classroom scene, he hides in his imagination. In many of its elements, the scene is a prototype for behavior that persists until the novel's final pages: in the association of heat with passions and external reality, and of coolness with

detachment and subjective ideality; in the imaginative
flight from the difficulty of a concrete situation; in the
numbing of the senses and the quieting of the body
that accompanies the contemplation of an aesthetic
image; and, finally, in the detachment from, and im-
provement on, the world accomplished by the particular
ideal image—in this case a green rose, which has never
been an object of perception and specifically represents
an imagined ideal: "But you could not have a green
rose. But perhaps somewhere in the world you could"
(*P,* p. 12). Eventually, a persistent gulf opens between
the subjective world and the outer world, and Stephen
soon prefers the "adventure in his mind." The tension
between the ideal and the real increases as Stephen
ages, with Stephen almost invariably perceiving reality
as hostile or ugly and attempting to deny it. Stephen's
most characteristic behavior in *Portrait* is subjective flight
from the world—by means of daydreams, perceptual
projections that reshape outer reality, pursuit of increasingly elusive ideals, or the controlled fantasies of art.

Stephen's tragicomic sexual history offers the most
pervasive and inclusive illustration of his double aliena-
tion from fleshly self and outer reality. That history,
furthermore, provides the necessary context for the
proper understanding of Stephen's aesthetic theories
and artistic practice. For that reason, I will briefly trace
its tortuous developments before examining the aesthetics and the composition of the villanelle in chapter five.

Sex, religion, and guilt first converge in Stephen's
young mind when his family prevents him from playing
with the Protestant Eileen whom he dreams of marry-
ing. Intense religious feeling then leads him to idealize
Eileen, as he does with E. C. later, through associating
her with the Blessed Virgin Mary. Eileen is the medium
for a divine revelation during a moment of blocked

vision when Stephen, his eyes covered by Eileen's hands, gains a sudden understanding of the Virgin Mary as a Tower of Ivory. The image of coolness, emblematic of detachment and idealization in the classroom scene, recurs here with reference not only to the ivorylike Virgin Mary, but also to Eileen, who has become for Stephen equally white, cool, and virginal—"a cold white thing." Unlike the "spiritual manifestations" of *Stephen Hero,* which reward profound, reposeful engagement with concrete matter, the spiritual manifestations of *Portrait* either transform, repudiate, or substitute for the concrete.

By the conclusion of chapter two, Stephen is incapable of conceiving of a flesh-and-blood woman who might receive and return love as well as physical passion. He has mentally reduced women to a few abstract types: temptresses to be resisted, whores to be used, and unblemished virgins to be adored and kept pure— sometimes with great difficulty, for they often enter into his erotic fantasies. His relations with women reflect the concepts he projects onto them, which themselves vary according to the circumstances. The woman has little reality in her own right, apart from her existence in Stephen's imagination. Thus, Emma has her innocence defiled and trampled on because of her role in Stephen's *imaginary* masturbatory orgies, and she shares in his sin and guilt when, in an outburst of religious fervor, he pictures himself *and Emma* called before the Virgin Mary for forgiveness. His tumultuous history of relations with women is prefigured early in the novel when Stephen recalls the white lavatory of the Wicklow Hotel. Contemplating the whiteness and the cold and hot cocks of the lavatory, Stephen himself flushes first cold, then hot. Stephen never escapes this pattern of alternating frigidity and warmth, of detach-

ment and passionate engagement, as the diary entry
for April 15 at the end of *Portrait* reveals. There, after
a brief encounter with E. C., he momentarily admits a
new feeling of affection for her; yet he had kept her
confused and at a distance, and his own feelings on ice,
when he "turned off that valve at once and opened
the spiritual-heroic refrigerating apparatus, invented
and patented in all countries by Dante Alighieri"
(*P,* p. 252).

Stephen often thwarts his boyish sexual impulses,
giving them no outlet in the world, but instead brooding
over an image of womanhood drawn from art—Mer-
cedes from *The Count of Monte Cristo.* At first, he
tries to realize "in the real world" his "unsubstantial
image" of woman, as he had earlier dreamed of finding
a green rose in the world. But reality cannot measure
up to his dreams, and he soon abandons the quest,
preferring the "adventure in his mind" (*P,* p. 78) and
the "company of phantasmal comrades" (*P,* p. 84).
Amid this chaos of frozen passions and idealized visions,
Stephen writes his first poem.

He has been to a children's party, where he held
himself aloof from the general merriment. But even
as he sat in willful isolation, flattering himself with his
superiority to his surroundings, a part of him wanted
to betray him into harmony with the world. E. C.,
especially, excited him with her glances. Nevertheless,
on the tram ride home from the party, Stephen resists
his impulse to hold and kiss E. C., despite her willingness for him to do so. He perceives her in a blend of
falsifying images: first, as a vaguely religious figure,
a nunlike innocent with a "cowled head"; then, on the
tram step below him, as a temptress trying to coax him
out of his protective isolation, down from his height.
The next day, Stephen re-creates the scene in a poem.

"By dint of brooding on the situation," Joyce writes, Stephen eliminates all those elements of it that "he deemed common and insignificant" (*P,* p. 70). The insignificant elements include, in fact, everything that is tangible—the tram, the horses, the tramman, E. C., and Stephen himself. All that remains are the darkness, a vague mood of longing, and a farewell between the disembodied lovers, who give the kiss that Stephen had withheld. Then, in a mixed mood of awe at his own poetic achievement and narcissistic self-sufficiency bordering on solipsism, Stephen goes into his mother's bedroom to gaze "at his face . . . in the mirror."

That Joyce gives us the content of the poem but nothing of its form forces us to consider Stephen's psychological processes. Perhaps the first thing to note is the influence of religion, which works from the novel's opening scene to draw Stephen out of the world. His religion teaches that human nature is corrupt; that his physical instincts are low, gross, and beastlike; and that the world is the snare of sin, likely to endanger his immortal soul for eternity unless he resists with a will. These ideas contribute to the psychological structure of the scene on the tram: the idea of E. C. as temptress, of the body's passions as something to keep coolly in check, of the world as a threat, of experience as a fall. Through his poem, Stephen maintains a state of grace by resisting the temptation to fall, yet vicariously gratifying that impulse, in a classic example of repression and sublimation. Finally, we should note the total absence of a direct and explicit relationship between experience and the work of art. Experience is the source for neither the content nor the images of the poem. Nor, strictly speaking, is the poem inspired by experience—it is the *non*-experience that inspires the poem; and the poem substitutes for lived experience, refining the human actors out of existence. Here art, like religious grace in chapter three, signifies experiential death.

The relationship between experience and art becomes a crucial issue later in the book. During his ecstatic experience in the presence of the "birdgirl" at the conclusion of chapter four, Stephen suddenly believes that his destiny is to be an artist who will "recreate life out of life." The phrase amounts to an artistic imperative that would require a radical metamorphosis of Stephen's character. Up to this point, he has avoided the warm passions of the world and the possible hell fire of the after world, through the device of withdrawing into the refrigerated atmosphere of his own imagination. Now he declares that his imagination will refract and transmute "the daily bread of experience" (*P*, p. 221). If he is to experience life, rather than flee it, as the antecedent to creative activity and as the source of his art's content and images, plainly he can no longer hold himself aloof on the top step of the tram. If the "artist struggles to express [beauty] from lumps of earth," to quote Stephen from a later scene, he must first know the earth. Stephen understands and accepts his obligation: "To live, to err, to fall, to triumph," he thinks joyously, eager to pass through the gates to the "fair courts of life." But we have heard this before, as we will again in Stephen's jubilant "Welcome O life" of the novel's final lines, and we have a right to suspect his new commitment to "life." The previous chapter, for example, ended similarly, with Stephen in a state of religious exaltation, following the purgations of the retreat, embracing the wondrous simplicity and beauty of "life," which "lay all before him." He congratulated himself on his new "life . . . of grace and virtue and happiness . . . not a dream from which he

would awake." Yet, within a few pages, his new life
was exposed as precisely that, a dream, another of the
"adventures of his mind." Nothing has occurred in the
interim to promise greater success in the future, except
for the vision of the "birdgirl." Yet the "birdgirl,"
whom Stephen perceives as the long-sought-for reali-
zation of his image of ideal woman in the real world,
is Stephen's Gerty MacDowell. In her white, ivorylike
pureness, she is an aesthetic image, an imposition on
the world, less experienced than created. Like Gretta
Conroy at the top of the stairs in Joyce's "The Dead,"
whom Gabriel enwraps with the garments that best
satisfy his own needs, the "birdgirl" is not perceived
for what she is, not interpreted with the "selective
faculty" of *Stephen Hero.* She is the mirror of Stephen's emotional state, the self-serving projection of
a doomed yearning. She is the natural descendant of
the imagined "harlots with gleaming jewel eyes," who
had previously stimulated Stephen's orgies of auto-
eroticism.

Chapter five demonstrates no new-found interest in
the palpable world, no fulfillment of Stephen's triumphant expectations on the beach in the previous chapter.
The opening paragraphs portray instead several brief
offenses to Stephen's sensibilities—the nagging of his
parents, the screeching of a mad nun, and the piles of
rubbish he must step over on his way to the university.
These cause Stephen a moment of bitterness and heart-
ache, but he quickly suppresses his feelings and turns
his mind away from the humiliations of the world.
Stephen's journey to the university parallels the morning tram ride to the university in *Stephen Hero,* which
I discussed in part one of this essay. In *Portrait,* however, Stephen does not arrange the trip to feel the wind
in his face, or to "partake in the morning life of the

city," or to observe the faces that he meets. Now indifferent to such experiences, his mind dwells instead
among the images of girls and moods remembered
from literature. In this way, Stephen escapes the degrading realities about him, which "pull his mind
downward" and provoke his anger. Every image from
the street turns his attention inward and evokes a recol-
lection from a given work of art—and thus "his soul"
is "loosed of her miseries" (*P,* p. 176). Despite his recent
commitment to the "fair courts of life," then, Stephen
persists in his world-weary scorn of the sensible environment and in his familiar dichotomy between flesh
and spirit. Stephen remains incapable of producing the
kind of art required by his own artistic mandate to
"recreate life out of life." Under the circumstances, his
art would not be nourished by life's experiences, but
by experience of other literature—not "life out of
life" but "art out of art." He would duplicate the
imaginative flight from the earth and the vicarious
fulfillment that he accomplished in his poem about
E. C. after the tram ride.

The whole of Stephen's prior history forms the inter-
pretive context for the aesthetics Stephen delivers to his
friend Lynch, a captive audience. Like the aesthetics
in *Stephen Hero,* those in *Portrait* are consistent with
Stephen's character and preceding activities. They illustrate Stephen's isolation, for instance, in that he shares
his ideas only with Lynch. The first Stephen had delivered his essay "Art and Life" to his University Literary and Historical Society, as Joyce himself had, and
had willingly talked about art with any relative or
acquaintance he could corner. More essential, however,
is that the emphasis throughout the discussion with
Lynch is on the divorcement of art from life and, in

the passages on aesthetic apprehension, on the subjective states of the perceiver.

Stephen begins with the assertion that "the proper arts" arrest the mind in a moment of stasis that transcends the kinetic emotions of desire and loathing. However persuasive or valid this idea might be in a different context—and it closely resembles Joyce's personal beliefs—Stephen's dictum that art must not excite desire needs to be interpreted in the light of his own life-long struggle to overcome desire and the tangible world. Assessed in terms of motives and consequences, Stephen's insistence on aesthetic stasis suggests that he craves, in art, an anodyne for his wounded senses and a refrigerating apparatus for his kinetic passions. Such are the effects, too, of Stephen's departure from Aristotle, whom he cites as his inspiration. Aristotle, of course, defined the effect of tragedy as the arousing of the emotions of pity and fear so as to accomplish their catharsis. But for Stephen, stasis is not the end result of a cathartic process; it is an arrestment that occurs simultaneously with perception. Moreover, he assumes a very doubtful division of mind and body and makes pity and fear states of *mind,* not emotion: "The *mind* is arrested and raised *above* desire and loathing" (*P,* p. 205, italics added). In the name of Aristotle, Stephen offers a Neoplatonic aesthetics in the tradition of Plotinus and Shelley, which postulates mental functioning in absolute detachment from physical drives. The aesthetic world, Stephen says, is "a mental world," free from the "gross earth" and its sensual stimuli, "which are the prison gates of the soul" (*P,* pp. 206–207).

Stephen regards disembodied spirituality as the condition proper to the creator of art as well as the

perceiver. In *Stephen Hero* he had declared that "art
is not an escape from life" and affirmed that the artist
creates "out of the fullness of his own life"—both
remarks implying that artistic activity is an expression
of the integrated, total man, who flourishes on the earth
(*SH,* p. 86). But on the beach in the birdgirl scene in
Portrait, Stephen looked forward to creating "out of
the freedom and power of [his] *soul*" (italics added).
Further, Stephen says that the artist, progressing from
lyric to dramatic forms, ultimately refines himself out
of existence, like the "indifferent" God of the creation,
or like Stephen himself after his tram ride with E. C.

When Stephen turns to his famous definition of
beauty and its apprehension, his emphasis remains on
the subjective states of the perceiver and his detachment
from the aesthetic object. In contrast with Joyce's own
early aesthetics, which carefully noted that "beauty is
a quality of something seen," beauty for Stephen is
another arrested mental state. Stephen begins with a
phrase from Aquinas, which he translates as "that is
beautiful the apprehension of which pleases" (*P,* p.
207). He places the stress on "apprehension" and
devotes several pages to its elaboration. In *Stephen
Hero,* the concepts of the "selective faculty" and the
"epiphany" had divided emphasis between the inner
gropings of the "spiritual eye" of the perceiver and the
external aesthetic object that the "spiritual eye" sought
to bring into exact focus. The act of aesthetic apprehension was reciprocal, a perception of beauty residing
in tangible form. But the absence of these concepts
from *Portrait* and the absence of the affirmation of the
"classical temper" result in a theory of aesthetic apprehension that describes the dimensions of the mind,
rather than of external objects, a spiritual eye now

turned inward and satisfied more by images of green roses than by Ballast Office clocks.

Immediately after delivering his lecture on aesthetics, Stephen encounters E. C. on the steps of the national library. He is as estranged from her now as he had been ten years before on the steps of the tram. He suspects her, perhaps wrongfully,[13] of a flirtation with a priest. He resents the fact that she would grant her intimacy to a "priested peasant" rather than to him. Yet, he holds her distant from him with his suspicions, his disdain, and his willed constraint of gestures that might promote intimacy. The truth is that he suspects and resists, not E. C., but the attraction he feels for her. She remains the temptress that she was ten years ago. Stephen now perceives her as "a figure of the womanhood of her country." Because Stephen no longer accepts the dogmas of religion, to yield would not now be a fall from grace into the snares of sin. Yet Irish Catholicism has left indelible traces on Stephen's being: despite his conscious repudiation of it, it controls his attitudes and his manner of thinking. To yield would still be a fall—of his proudly innocent soul from its frosty heights, into warmly passionate relationship with a woman in the concrete world. Just such a fall is called for by Stephen's recent commitment "to live, to err, to fall, to triumph, to recreate life out of life" (*P,* p. 172). But the risk of injury and pain, of humiliation, loss, and failure, is too great. Instead, as he had ten years earlier, Stephen retires to his room to write a poem.[14]

Stephen's villanelle duplicates the psychological processes of his earlier poem and reveals him at his most Platonic and romantic. Despite his self-proclaimed intention of "transmuting the daily bread of experience" into art, his villanelle has as its inspiration a

"vision" of "the ecstasy of seraphic life" (*P,* p. 217).
Stephen has held himself apart from E. C. in the previous scene, but he cannot eradicate the deep-rooted
need for human relationship. He experiences that desire
as a feeling of imprisonment and an impulse toward
flight. During the night before the composition of the
villanelle, he has escaped his isolation in a dream,
through spiritual union with angels and the Holy Ghost.
Upon awakening, still bathed in the afterglow of his
dream-vision, he suddenly feels the Holy Ghost descend
to him, a spirit he inbreathes "passionlessly." This is
not the Holy Ghost of the church, of course, but the
analogous figure in Stephen's new religion of art. Appro-
priately enough, therefore, the "Holy Spirit" appears
amid images of flame and luminous clouds and brings
Stephen a kind of "gift of tongues"—the ability to
articulate his poem. His lips begin to murmur the
rhythms of the villanelle, as though God were working
through him, God's mere agent. A burning glow within
his spirit purges the world of passions—"Its rays
burned up the world, consumed the hearts of men and
angels"—including both the "willful heart" of Stephen's
temptress and his own restless heart. By composing the
poem, then, Stephen extends the feeling of liberation
achieved during the night's dream-vision. He momentarily rids himself of desire and loathing, arrests and
raises his mind above his kinetic passions. From this
elevated vantage point, he can indulge a fleeting view
of E. C. with greater sympathy: "He began to feel that
he had wronged her. A sense of her innocence moved
him almost to pity her" (*P,* p. 222). But his sympathy
indicates no clearer perception of the "real" E. C., or
any deeper understanding of her. For no sooner has
Stephen excused her from personal blame, than he
affirms the collective guilt she bears merely for being

a woman: "the strange humiliation of her nature . . . the dark shame of womanhood." Stephen's obscure language apparently describes menstruation, as the outward sign of female sexuality, and vividly demonstrates that, in Stephen's Irish Catholic mind, the "figure of womanhood" remains threatening and vaguely evil, the "weaker vessel" of tradition.

Thinking of "the dark shame of womanhood," Stephen feels a rekindled desire in his "soul." He resumes composition of the poem, contemplating all the while the nakedness of a female "soul" awakening in response to his own desire. The soul of the temptress of the villanelle, his ostensible concern, blends at this point with the imagined picture of E. C. In his imagination, the composite naked soul yields to him and does so in quite explicitly *physical* terms—the soul now possesses warmth, odor, dark languorous eyes, and lavish limbs. With her submission, Stephen is free to complete his poem. The poem signifies the successful sublimation of his desire, its conversion first into an amorphous spiritual force and ultimately into the poem itself. To Stephen's conscious understanding, the submission of the temptress represents his overmastering of a recalcitrant "figure of womanhood"; E. C., whom he has "purified in and reprojected from" his imagination, is elevated from life into art. To us, who see more than Stephen does, the submission of the temptress is the symbolic fulfillment of his suppressed desire, the achievement in art of what he has denied himself in life. The villanelle, like Stephen's poem ten years earlier, momentarily pacifies the demands of the flesh through a symbolic masturbation and thus enables Stephen to sustain his detachment from the world and his posture of superiority.[15]

The villanelle grants a temporary respite from the

romantic *Weltschmerz* that Stephen exudes after composing the first five stanzas of the poem: "All around him life was about to awaken in common noises, hoarse voices, sleepy prayers. Shrinking from that life he turned towards the wall, making a cowl of the blanket and staring at the great overblown scarlet flowers of the tattered wallpaper. He tried to warm his perishing joy in their scarlet glow, imagining a roseway from where he lay upwards to heaven all strewn with scarlet flowers. Weary! Weary! He too was weary of ardent ways" (*P*, pp. 221–222). Here is the truth of Stephen's spiritual transcendence and arrested mind: a rose-strewn pathway to heaven, another dream, another adventure of his mind. The Dublin minotaur has affronted Stephen and piqued him into healthy flight. But it has crippled him, wounded him so deeply that he is incapable of genuine escape, as opposed to mere escapism. He is trapped in a perpetual cycle: the dream of illusory liberty followed inevitably by the humiliating puncture of the dream—for reality validates itself and cannot be denied indefinitely.

The composition of the villanelle perfectly illustrates what both Joyce and *Stephen Hero* call the "spiritual anarchy" of the "impatient romantic temper." It illustrates, too, Freud's early and reductive conception of artistic activity as escape from "reality" through "substitute gratification." Like his religion, Stephen's art leads him out of the world. But the way out of the labyrinth of the mind leads back to earth, not to heaven. This can result from a different kind of—I would say genuine—creative activity: the aesthetic principles advocated by the youthful Joyce and practiced by the mature Joyce, those elaborated in *Stephen Hero* and paid lip service to by Stephen in *Portrait* in the phrase "recreate life out of life." Authentic personal freedom and spiritual growth will follow for Stephen only when he first turns to the things of the world—to perceive their intelligibility and penetrate to their significance, their "meaning which is still unuttered," in the words of *Stephen Hero*. As Stephen's mother says just before the book's end, he needs to learn "what the heart is and what it feels," rather than "consume" it in art. Stephen's apparent acceptance of her judgment is mere glibness: "Amen. So be it. Welcome, O life!" As both Stephen and Leopold Bloom discover in *Ulysses,* the acceptance of "life" is not so simple and painless.

But we need not look forward to *Ulysses* to hear the hollowness in Stephen's phrase. Two entries in Stephen's book-concluding diary adumbrate his future disappointment by emphasizing his continuing immaturity. On April 6, Stephen compares himself to Yeats's Michael Robartes, who longs for forgotten beauty "long faded from the world." In contrast, Stephen's yearning is for "the loveliness which has not yet come into the world." He still pursues a green rose, which can be found neither in Ireland nor in France nor in any far corner of the "fair courts of life," but only in his own subjective imagination. On April 15, Stephen again reveals that, on the brink of voluntary exile, he remains incapable of living in the world as part of it. He meets E. C., but keeps her safely outside the perimeter of his being by opening "the spiritual-heroic refrigerating apparatus." Later, alone, he admits: "I liked her today. . . . I liked her and it seems a new feeling for me." But poised as he is for Daedalian flight, Stephen cannot face the implications of his new feeling: "Then, in that case, all the rest, all that I thought I thought and all that I felt I felt, all the rest before now, in fact . . . O, give it up, old chap! Sleep it off!" (*P,* p. 252).

His next diary entry reads, "Away! Away!" His flight,

130 | Charles Rossman

premised on his numbing of passion and willful avoid-
ance of self-knowledge, is Stephen's last work of art
in *Portrait*. Like his two poems, his flight is an attempt
at spiritual transcendence founded on suppressed physical realities. Consequently, his future is augured in the
prideful fall of Icarus, the true "bird of augury," whom
Stephen figuratively becomes in the novel's final line:
"Old father, old artificer, stand me now and ever in
good stead."

Notes

1. Hugh Kenner, *Dublin's Joyce* (Boston: Beacon Press,
1962), p. 120.

2. S. L. Goldberg, *The Classical Temper* (London: Chatto
and Windus, 1963), pp. 41–65.

3. Robert Scholes, "Joyce and the Epiphany: The Key to
the Labyrinth?" *Sewanee Review* 72 (1964): 70. Scholes has
elaborated his view of the epiphany and the relative maturity
of Stephen in a number of publications, including an article
in *Texas Studies in Language and Literature* 3, no. 1 (Spring
1961): 8–15, in which he argues that Joyce intends Stephen
to triumph at the end of *Portrait;* a rebuttal to Florence Walzl
in *PMLA* 82 (1967): 152–154, where he insists that the term
epiphany should be applied only to the seventy-odd epiphanies
Joyce wrote before 1904; and his two volumes *The Workshop
of Daedalus* and the Viking Critical Edition of *Dubliners.*

4. Ellsworth Mason and Richard Ellmann, eds., *The Critical Writings of James Joyce* (New York: Viking Press,
1964), p. 45. Hereafter cited in the text as *CW*.

5. Richard Ellmann, ed., *Letters of James Joyce,* II, 134.

6. The phrase is from J. A. Smith's translation of *De Anima,*
vol. 3 (1931), of *The Works of Aristotle,* ed. J. A. Smith
and W. D. Ross (Oxford: Clarendon Press, 1910–1952).

7. James Joyce, *Stephen Hero* (New York: New Directions,
1963), p. 30. Hereafter cited in the text as *SH*.

8. Scholes, "Joyce and the Epiphany," p. 70.

9. See especially William York Tindall, *James Joyce: His*

Way of Interpreting the Modern World (New York: Scribner's, 1950), pp. 16–17; but this view permeates the book and his later book as well: *A Reader's Guide to James Joyce* (New York: Noonday Press, 1959).

10. James Joyce, *Ulysses* (New York: The Modern Library, 1961), p. 589.

11. Kenner, *Dublin's Joyce,* p. 112.

12. James Joyce, *A Portrait of the Artist as a Young Man* (New York: Viking Press, 1964), p. 48. Hereafter cited in the text as *P.*

13. See *Portrait,* p. 202, where Davin tells Stephen "that's all in your mind."

14. Stephen's villanelle has elicited surprisingly few direct commentaries from Joyce's critics. Kenner regards the poem as "Frenchified verses" written "in bed in an erotic swoon" (*Dublin's Joyce,* p. 112). Tindall throughout his *Reader's Guide* treats the poem as evidence of Stephen's pretensions. Wayne Booth discusses the poem in his *The Rhetoric of Fiction* as part of a general discussion of aesthetic "distance" in *Portrait* and concludes that Joyce has damaged the novel by leaving readers uncertain about how to respond to the poem. Robert Scholes has responded to Booth (*PMLA* 79, [1964]: 484–489) with a sensitive reading of the whole episode of the villanelle, arguing that Joyce means to depict a serious and noteworthy example of Stephen's art. Plainly, the issues are too complex for adequate treatment here, and my observations are not meant to be a full-blown analysis of the poem.

15. Two recent interpretations of the villanelle episode interpret the submission of E. C. in different ways: Edward Brandabur understands it as symbolic fulfillment of a sexual desire (*The Celtic Cross,* ed. Ray Browne [Purdue University Press, 1964]). Maurice Beebe, in the same volume (p. 25), regards it as an example of transmuting the daily bread of experience.

SIX

Virginia Woolf:
Tradition and
Modernity

Avrom Fleishman

CRITICS have been kind to Virginia Woolf, but there is little literary criticism to show for it. Few literary scholars would pursue to book length an exclusively psychological, philosophical, or linguistic study of other great modern writers. Exceptions will, of course, come to mind: there exist single-minded psychoanalytic studies of Conrad, philosophical studies of Eliot, and linguistic studies of Joyce—each in its own way reducing the writer's art to something out of which it is made. But such studies have been the rule, rather than the exception, among recent books on Woolf. It is time for literary criticism to function, if Woolf is to be seen as one of the few transcendent modern masters.

As Woolf is not only the contemporary, but at some points the literary confrère, of Eliot, Joyce, Pound, and Yeats, it is not surprising that her imagination worked in much the same way as theirs. Hers is a fundamentally literary sensibility: she is a creature of books. Generated by her father, Leslie Stephen, and his library, sustained by constant reviewing for the *Times Literary Supplement* and other periodicals, at home in a notoriously bookish milieu, Woolf lived her life in the marketplace of literary ideas and objects. Into that forum went the classics, all of English literature, and the contemporary outpouring—good, bad, and in limbo. Constantly educating herself—and chafing at being deprived, as a woman, of a solid classical education—Woolf became a *learned* author; not in Milton's sense, perhaps, but at least in Arnold's.

This life-long bout of reading was to lead Woolf to weave her works out of metaphors, allusions, and quotations drawn from the classics—ancient and modern. In composing a train of verbal associations, she makes a synthesis of the sentiments, values, and perceptions of her tradition; she incorporates Sophocles, Montaigne, Shakespeare, and much, much else into her sensibility. The signs of this assimilation are to be found not only in works of parodic cultural history like *Orlando* and *Between the Acts,* but also in everything she wrote. This synthesis is apparent in the very tissue of her mind, which she held to be a function of all the minds with which she had come into contact—in books as well as in life. More radical than Eliot's theory of "tradition and the individual talent," less artificial than Yeats's notions of the artist's use of his predecessors as masks from which to shape his identity, Woolf's view of the artist's culture was drawn from her own experience in furnishing the chambers of her mind. And that view led her—as similar views led Eliot, Yeats, Pound, and Joyce—to practice what may be called the encyclopedic style: the network of allusion that stands as the dominant mode in modern British literature.

To place Woolf in this company is not intended merely to bestow accolades but to establish an appropriate context for reading her works. As it is with novelists like Fielding or George Eliot, it is important to know what Woolf read and what she thought of it as she formed her own ideas of fiction. But to set up an intellectual context—as is by now well known—is only preliminary to the criticism of individual works of art, in which learned background is made aesthetic foreground. At the very least, a scholarly criticism would discover the sources and determine the relevance of Woolf's numerous quotations and references—a task that has been left largely undone. By following up the words of the text, one finds their meanings in all sorts of recondite and not-so-recondite places, and one can then bring the original literary sources to bear on the meaning of the work of art at hand. The critical procedure is not very different from that which we use for Joyce or Pound, and it is perhaps only a difference of degree that distinguishes the approach from that which we take to premodern nonencyclopedic authors. Yet differences of degree or quantity pass over into differences of quality or kind, and it is this quality of referential abundance that marks literary encyclopedism.

When the emphasis on literary allusion becomes highly pronounced, it becomes harder to speak of a prose fiction as a novel in any pre-Joycian sense. In reading the major modern authors, we have come to expect generic innovation as a mark of modernity, but in Woolf the strength of tradition shifts the direction of her experiments from novelty per se to a manipulation of the données of genre. One obvious gambit is to speak of her novels as "poetic," but Woolf sought a more precise term to describe her experiments in genre: "I have an idea that I will invent a new name for my books to supplant 'novel.' A new ——— by Virginia Woolf. But what? Elegy?" [1] Elegy is a poetic genre, of course, but it functions in Woolf's fiction as an end—remembrance and propitiation of the dead—rather than as a set of conventional means. And it functions only in certain Woolf fictions, not in others: elegy is most in evidence in *Jacob's Room* and *To the Lighthouse,* which evoke Woolf's brother and parents, respectively. *Orlando* is, of course, subtitled *A Biography,* and operates as a conspicuous parody of that genre throughout—or, if not of the genre itself, of its standard practitioners. Other cases are harder to specify, but it could be contended—given more time than I now have—that *The Waves* is organized on the model of a creation myth, rich in references to Genesis, while *Between the Acts* moves toward a high form of drama, incorporating theatrical conventions, history, and simulated slices of contemporary life. It would be best to speak of Woolf's works severally as novel-drama, novel-biography, or novel-elegy, but in the absence of general agreement on these designations I shall refer to them neutrally as "fictions."

Virginia Woolf's first substantial fiction, *The Voyage Out,* is structured on the model of two classic *mythoi*— the journey and the initiation. Yet *The Voyage Out* is not a mythological novel of the kind that was to become a major strain in modern fiction, a strain with which later Woolf fictions will be found to be linked. The familiar theme of a young English girl's development is here given greater universality by being treated as a journey in quest, her social maturation and growth of consciousness are deepened by relating them to so-called primitive patterns of initiation, and her experience of love and death is set in a landscape of primal nature—the Amazon, oddly enough.

Acting to enrich this mingling of the archetypal and

the familiar is a series of quotations from literary works
of all sorts. As are many of the fictions to follow in the
Woolf canon, this is a literary work about a literary
world—literature forming part of the substance of its
characters and an element of its narrative mode of portraying them. The array of quotes is, moreover, highly
relevant to one of the work's main preoccupations. In
line with its treatment of a young girl's education, *The
Voyage Out* follows her (Rachel) in a short course in
western literature, thereby conveying her cultural as
well as emotional growth. Much of the conversation on
ship and at the villa is concerned with the questions of
what to read, what to make of one's reading, and what
value to assign to one's books. Indeed, the choice of
reading matter becomes an index of character, as the
several major and minor characters are established
chiefly by the accounts they give of their literary taste
and experience. They range from the omnivorous Miss
Allen, who marshals a host of stock phrases to compose
her survey of English literature, to the iconoclastic Mrs.
Flushing, who remains aloof from the literary chitchat
until a young man shows her a scurrilous passage of
Swinburne. But the main interest is in the development
of a heroine, and it is consequently her reading that is
most closely followed—particularly focusing on works
that direct her attention to what will be the central
experiences of her brief life—love and death.

To sum up Rachel's course of reading: she drops an
awkward translation of *Tristan and Isolde* to pick up
"Cowper's Letters, the classic prescribed by her father
which had bored her," [2] but this reversion to safe,
paternal paths is short-lived. She turns to *Wuthering
Heights* (*VO,* pp. 61, 83), like *Tristan* a tale of love
impossible under the conditions of earthly life and ful-
filling itself only in death, but one mediated by a more

complex and less morbidly romantic perspective.
Clarissa Dalloway, who first appears in *The Voyage
Out,* next exposes Rachel to another version of transcendence in death, Shelley's "Adonais," quoting from
lines 352–356:

> He has outsoared the shadow of our night,
> Envy and calumny and hate and pain—
>
> .   .   .   .
>
> Can touch him not and torture not again
> From the contagion of the world's slow stain.
>
> (*VO,* p. 62)

The effect of these lines on Rachel is unclear; she
does not take to reading Shelley, but the association of
love and death is further established as a prefiguration
of her career. Rachel does, however, respond to another
of Mrs. Dalloway's suggestions: to read Jane Austen.
Rachel is initially prejudiced against her as being "so
like a tight plait" (*VO,* p. 62), but is somewhat en-
couraged by Mr. Dalloway's pronouncement that
Austen is "incomparably the greatest female writer we
possess . . . and for this reason: she does not attempt to
write like a man" (*VO,* p. 66); however, Clarissa immediately reveals that Austen "always sends [Dalloway]
to sleep!" (*VO,* p. 67). But though Dalloway does
doze off after a few lines of *Persuasion* are quoted (*VO,*
p. 67), Rachel's attention to a writer who can help her
define her own feminine identity is aroused. Her subsequent dalliance with Dalloway is ironically accompanied by his recommendation to read Burke, just before he snatches a kiss from her (*VO,* p. 84), but their
relationship returns to the aegis of Austen as it closes:
when the Dalloways leave the ship Clarissa's parting
gift is a copy of *Persuasion* (*VO,* p. 87).

It does not appear that Rachel reads the novel, although the charm of the Dalloways persists and leads her to ask her uncle for Burke's *"Speech on the American Revolution"* (*VO,* p. 202). The shift in her taste toward the eighteenth century is abetted by meeting St. John Hirst, who recommends Gibbon and sends her the first volume of the *Decline and Fall* (*VO,* p. 203), but she concludes that she has been "horribly, oh infernally, damnably bored" (*VO,* p. 251). Meanwhile, she picks up other works of fiction (Balzac's *Cousine Bette: VO,* p. 202) and drama (Ibsen's *Doll's House: VO,* pp. 142–143), but the value of her literary experience is judged when she brings it to bear on her first romantic challenge: "none of the books she read, from *Wuthering Heights* to *Man and Superman,* and the plays of Ibsen, suggested from their analysis of love that what their heroines felt was what she was feeling now" (*VO,* p. 272).

While Rachel develops her literary taste, in line with her larger course of development, the cultural atmosphere around her is slowly established. It is the culture of the English middle classes, firmly classicist in its bettereducated strata. From the outset of the voyage, we are greeted by the marks of high culture in the name of the ship: the *Euphrosyne*—one of the Graces, whose name is associated with happiness. Shipboard conversation is dominated by the presence of the professional classicist, Ridley Ambrose—who is working on an edition of Pindar that has long ago reached at least three volumes and who has also published a "commentary on Aristotle" (*VO,* p. 20)—and his Cambridge crony, the apparently nonprofessional scholar Pepper, who "devoted January to Petronius, February to Catullus, March to the Etruscan vases perhaps" (*VO,* p. 21).

Their learning is not a salient element in the story, except at one point: when the Dalloways come aboard and are being introduced to the company, Clarissa puts on her little act of admiration for the classics, and Pepper strikes up with a quotation from the *Antigone,* which is given in the original Greek in the fictional text. In R. C. Jebb's translation, these lines (lines 332–335) from the famous chorus on man run: "Wonders are many, and none is more wonderful than man; the power that crosses the white sea, driven by the stormy south wind, making a path under surges that threaten to engulf him." The lines are well chosen, of course, as a snatch of mellifluous Greek and have an appropriate relation to the setting in which the party of sea voyagers finds itself. But Pepper does not go on to quote the rest of the chorus, which Jebb summarizes as follows: "Man is master of sea and land; he subdues all other creatures; he has equipped his life with all resources, except a remedy for death." (At the end of this chorus, Antigone is brought in to face Creon and, eventually, her doom.)[3] For those on ship or off with a knowledge of the chorus's import, it would act as a premonition of an ultimate fatality, as well as a congratulation on an adventurous voyage. To put the matter in thematic terms, the citation from the Greek serves to universalize the novel's action as a voyage of human enterprise and make it a symbol of the passage of life toward death. Other prefigurations of death in underwater imagery occur on the ocean voyage, as the steward, Mr. Grice, quotes, "Full fathom five thy father lies" (*VO,* p. 57), and this pattern of imagery maintains throughout the work a close association with the heroine's movement toward death.

In similar fashion, the hero of the tale acquires a grasp of his experience through the medium of literature, while the reader simultaneously sees the action in

its larger, archetypal form. We find Terence Hewet
reading Hardy, Whitman, and Milton, each with reference to his personal preoccupations. He first quotes the
final stanza of Hardy's "He Abjures Love," from *Time's
Laughingstocks:*

> I speak as one who plumbs
>   Life's dim profound,
> One who at length can sound
>   Clear views and certain.
> But—after love what comes?
>   A scene that lours,
> A few sad vacant hours,
>   And then, the Curtain.

(VO, p. 127)

Hewet is a young man weighing his hopes and prospects
in love, and the Hardian bitterness of abjuration comes
readily to him, even though not yet tested by experience. But there is also in the quotation a premonition
of death and the emptiness of life after love (in the
poem, to be sure, the anticipated death is that of the
abjuring lover rather than of the beloved). Moreover,
a number of earlier lines that Hewet fails to quote
have a subsequent relevance to Rachel's death by fever
and to his own desolation: "But lo, Love beckoned me.
And I was bare, / And poor, and starved, and dry, /
And fever-stricken." We may take his prescience in
selecting this poem as typical of the thematic working
of *The Voyage Out:* it repeatedly introduces the notes
of love and death in close conjunction, especially in
literary contexts, before they are brought together in
the protagonists' experience.

Terence's next burst of poetry occurs on the river
journey:

Whoever you are holding me now in [your] hand,
Without one thing all will be useless.

(VO, p. 327)

This is Whitman, giving fair warning to the universe
of his ineradicable individuality—"I give you fair warning before you attempt me further, / I am not what
you supposed, but far different"—in a poem from
Calamus that draws its title from the first line (which
Terence misquotes by adding the bracketed word indicated above). Terence presumably would refer this
evocation of the one thing needful to Rachel, of whom
he is thinking while reading, but in the context of the
novel's journeyings it would seem to have a range of
reference commensurate with Whitman's own: "Carry
me when you go forth over land or seas." Hewet has
been experiencing a sense of passage from the known
to the unknown, finding it "useless for him to struggle
any longer with the irresistible force of his own feelings.
He was drawn on and on away from all he knew . . ."
(*VO,* p. 326). The poetic utterance here serves to underscore a movement of heightened life to which
Hewet, like Rachel, is led in the course of the journey,
both by the force of love and by the hovering presence
of death.

The final expression of Terence's poetic strain is his
use of a well-known lovely lyric in the course of his
wooing of Rachel. He reads to her from "Comus":

There is a gentle nymph not far from hence,
That with moist curb sways the smooth Severn stream.
Sabrina is her name, a virgin pure; . . .

(VO, p. 398)

After quoting this description of the tutelary deity, he
goes on to read the song that calls her forth in the
masque:

> Sabrina fair,
>> Listen where thou art sitting
>> Under the glassy, cool, translucent wave,
>
> .   .   .   .
>
>> Goddess of the silver lake,
>> Listen and save!
>
> *(VO,* p. 399)

In the ongoing action of the novel, Rachel responds by noting the first signs of her illness: she feels hot, her head aches, and she can hardly bring herself to the effort of interrupting the reading. In this context, then, the famous song points the irony of Rachel's demise: she, too, has been a virgin wooed on the river, but, instead of coming to "listen and save," she goes down to her death.[4]

The final quotations of poetry are made by Ridley Ambrose and appear to be merely rhythmic aids to his pacing, while passing the time waiting for Rachel to die:

> Peor and Baalim
> Forsake their Temples dim,
>> With that twice batter'd God of Palestine
> And mooned Astaroth—
>
> *(VO,* p. 428)

These lines from Milton's ode "On the Morning of Christ's Nativity" (lines 197–200) prove, however, not merely rhythmical (like the ballad-meter lines he speaks on p. 427) but functional. They refer to the triumph of the new dispensation over the pagan gods of the East—but they come into the fiction at a singularly unconvincing moment, at the point of Rachel's dissolution. There is no hint of resurrection or of any other form of transcendence at the close; the blank

fact of death alone remains, as Hewet is led away from
the dead body with which he seemed to be in communication, and as the rhythm of daily life picks up
again at the hotel.

Virginia Woolf's second fiction, also critically slighted
and little read, is a fairly conventional love story told
in the form of an extended variation on the pattern of
Shakespearian romantic comedy. The interest of *Night
and Day* is more in its manipulation of conventions
than in its characters or themes, but the remarkable
effect of these manipulations is that convention becomes
thematic and revelatory in its own right. Under this
treatment, a tale of middle-class mating habits reaches
to depths of consciousness and communication that
approach those of Woolf's later fiction.

Shakespeare's presence in *Night and Day*—by direct
reference, thematic analogue, and parodic echo—is
strong enough to make this a prime instance of literature about literature—a record of one major artist's
confrontation with another. This literary self-consciousness is not, as has been claimed, enmeshed in a return
to the realistic conventions of nineteenth-century novels.
Those critics who tend to dismiss it as a relapse into a
fin-de-siècle style miss the chance to catch it in an even
more radical reversion. In writing a fictional romance,
Woolf attempts to rework the generic themes of illusion
and reality, the compact of lunatic, lover and poet, and
the miraculous transforming power of love.[5]

In other Woolf fictions, quotations from Shakespeare
are made the focus of dramatic scenes—as with "Sonnet
98" in *To the Lighthouse*—or become thematic by in-
sistent repetition—as does the dirge from *Cymbeline*
in *Mrs. Dalloway.* In *Night and Day,* no one Shakespearian element is allowed to predominate: plot, char-

acter, even thematic structure are invaded by the bardic presence.

It has been generally observed that the work's title establishes a duality between a night world of love and imagination opposed to a day world of mundane contemporary reality. The fact that several Shakespearian comedies are organized around this polarity—with two of them incorporating the image of night in their titles —suggests that the fiction's dual structure is itself a derivation from Shakespeare.

The formula for the action is equally familiar: beginning with two pairs of lovers, we find one couple (Katharine Hilbery and William Rodney) unstably engaged, while the other is fractured by its relationship to the first (Mary Datchet loves Ralph Denham, but, instead of returning her love, he loves Katharine). Such an imbroglio has been manipulated in romantic comedy in a number of ways, and the pattern Woolf chose was one that might be called the shuffle: a new character is introduced, causing a realignment of relations, with one of the original members left out in the cold.

As it is in the geometrical arrangement of relationships and in the formal balance of themes, the presence of Shakespeare is also felt throughout the text in a series of references to his life, works, and symbolic lordship over art and love. Not only Katharine's mother but also her aunt, Mrs. Cosham, are his devotees. Their perpetual reference to him is initially placed within a satire of their late-Victorian, "arty" aestheticism, but the characterization of Mrs. Hilbery's Shakespearianism comes to mean much more than this topical satire suggests.

At first Woolf's characterization serves to bolster the impression of Mrs. Hilbery as an effectual poetaster, busily failing to write the biography of her father, the great poet "Richard Alardyce." As late as chapter 24, this characterization is maintained with amusing simplicity, but at that point Mrs. Hilbery's significance begins to be complicated, in association with a more complex account of her interest in Shakespeare:

> Even Katharine was slightly affected against her better judgment by her mother's enthusiasm. Not that her judgment could altogether acquiesce in the necessity for a study of Shakespeare's sonnets as a preliminary to the fifth chapter of her grandfather's biography. Beginning with a perfectly frivolous jest, Mrs. Hilbery had evolved a theory that Anne Hathaway had a way, among other things, of writing Shakespeare's sonnets; . . . she had come half to believe in her joke, which was, she said, at least as good as other people's facts, and all her fancy for the time being centered upon Stratford-on-Avon. She had a plan . . . for visiting Shakespeare's tomb. Any fact about the poet had become, for the moment, of far greater interest to her than the immediate present.[6] (*ND*, p. 322)

That this idolatry carries a hint of the mystical, as well as a touch of the ridiculous, is suggested by her wish to set up as a prophet in the street, commanding: "People, read Shakespeare!" (*ND*, p. 323). She also announces her own relationship to Shakespeare's characters and thereby prepares for her dramatic and mythic role in the denouement of the love plot: "Your father's Hamlet, come to years of discretion: and I'm—well, I'm a bit of them all; I'm quite a large bit of the fool, but the fools in Shakespeare say all the clever things" (*ND*, p. 324). As Mrs. Hilbery rattles on, trying to find a particular quotation in Shakespeare about love, her fantasy comes to infect the sober, rational mind of her daughter, so that Katharine begins to wool-gather at her work and comes to feel that "a quotation from Shakespeare would not have come amiss" (*ND,* p. 326).

Mrs. Hilbery fulfills her intention to visit the Shakespeare country, explaining: "I've been dreaming all night of you and Shakespeare, dearest Katharine" (*ND,* p. 453). When she returns, at the final arrangement in the lovers' reshuffling, she appears surrounded with Shakespearian attributes that effectively transform her from a mere object of satire into a master of festivities. In archetypal terms, she plays the role of fairy godmother or cook-doctor who arranges the lovers' union and removes all obstacles in their path (in this case, the blocking action of her husband, who is disturbed by the lovers' departure from "civilization" in abruptly changing their engagements). Mrs. Hilbery's theatrical re-entrance is accompanied by floral arrangements that establish her ritual role as sanctifier of fertility: " 'From Shakespeare's tomb!' exclaimed Mrs. Hilbery, dropping the entire mass upon the floor, with a gesture that seemed to indicate an act of dedication. Then she flung her arms wide and embraced her daughter" (*ND,* p. 508). When Katharine expresses her distrust of the feelings she and Ralph share—"an illusion—as if when we think we're in love we make it up—we imagine what doesn't exist" (*ND,* p. 513)—Mrs. Hilbery answers with authority: "We have to have faith in our vision. . . . Believe me, Katharine, it's the same for every one—for me, too—for your father." In response to this manifestation of universal, if not divine, authority, "Katharine looked at her as if, indeed, she were some magician." And Mrs. Hilbery only partly returns to the realistic mode as the scene closes: "She swept up her flowers, breathed in their sweetness, and, humming a little song about a miller's daughter, left the room."

Mrs. Hilbery's regenerative comedy becomes an active force as she performs her office of bringing the lovers together—literally collecting them from various parts of London in her carriage. The bodily assemblage is accompanied by a ritualistic instruction in her Shakespearian doctrines: "She went on talking; she talked, it seemed to both the young men, to some one outside, up in the air. She talked about Shakespeare, she apostrophized the human race, she proclaimed the virtues of divine poetry, she began to recite verses which broke down in the middle" (*ND,* p. 520). Although the burden of this mystery is never made clear, it is nonetheless effective for those whom she instructs: "The gesture with which she dismissed him had a dignity that Ralph never forgot. She seemed to make him free with a wave of her hand to all that she possessed" (*ND,* p. 520). The fullest revelation of her tutelage is made when she croons over the united lovers: "she did nothing but talk about Shakespeare's tomb. 'So much earth and so much water and that sublime spirit brooding over it all,' she mused, and went on to sing her strange, half-earthly song of dawns and sunsets, of great poets, and the unchanged spirit of noble loving which they had taught, so that nothing changes, and one age is linked with another, and no one dies, and we all meet in spirit, until she appeared oblivious of any one in the room" (*ND,* p. 526). Here in parodic form is an initial statement of some of the themes of cultural continuity, loving communication, and apparent transcendence of death that are to dominate Woolf's later fiction.

The effect of Shakespeare's name on Katharine is appropriate to one whose life is being invaded by the spirit of romantic comedy: "All this talk about Shakespeare had acted as a soporific, or rather as an incantation upon Katharine" (*ND*, p. 529). The magic charm works, and in their closing embrace the lovers are surrounded by elements of an Elizabethan finale or masque: "they had been borne on, victors in the forefront of some triumphal car, spectators of a pageant enacted for them, masters of life" (*ND*, p. 532). There is an even more marked acquisition of Shakespearian attributes as their thoughts turn to the future: " 'As you like,' she replied. . . . it seemed to her that the immense riddle was answered; the problem had been solved; she held in her hands for one brief moment the globe which we spend our lives in trying to shape, round, whole, and entire from the confusion of chaos" (*ND*, p. 533). Here the language and imagery of two key Shakespearian principles are brought to the service of these modern lovers: "as you like" as a principle of comic freedom and the world as a globe that can be encompassed by art and love.

Like Shakespearian festive comedies in which an interruption of ordinary life allows the exceptional to emerge, *Night and Day* is a comedy of transformation under the spell of the illusions of love. That these illusions are continuous with the illusions fostered by art and that illusion is here not error but a means of access to certain realities unavailable to ordinary experience —these themes in Woolf's fiction owe much of their substance to Shakespeare. And the trials, illuminations, and purgations worked out in the plot, the range in mode from social satire to mysterious suggestions of sorcery, the underlying links to ritual and archetypal patterns—all operate in the fiction much as they have been shown by modern criticism to do in Shakespearian drama. Just as some of the more practical characters look askance at the star-struck behavior of the lovers, we too may find this the story of a "season of lunacy" (*ND*, p. 436)—and find it all the more acceptable because of it. In this context, the fiction can be seen as adumbrating an apocalyptic vision of personal happiness, social unity, and racial regeneration at the ritual meal that celebrates the lovers' union: "before the meal was far advanced civilization had triumphed, and Mr. Hilbery presided over a feast which came to wear more and more surely an aspect, cheerful, dignified, promising well for the future" (*ND,* p. 531).

The image of Shakespeare also figures strongly in *Mrs. Dalloway,* although it does not have the central position that it takes in *Night and Day.* Clarissa Dalloway alternates between quotations from *Cymbeline* and *Othello* as expressions of her tendencies toward life and death, respectively: "Fear no more the heat of the sun" (act 4, scene 2); "If it were now to die, / 'Twere now to be most happy" (act 2, scene 1). Septimus Smith, the secondary focus of the work, is also defined in terms of Shakespeare; he has been imaginatively formed by "the intoxication of language— *Antony and Cleopatra*" (*MD,* p. 98). Even in his approach to suicide, this inspiration persists: "He was not afraid. At every moment Nature signified[,] . . . standing close up to breathe through her hollowed hands Shakespeare's words, her meaning" (*MD,* p. 154). By the same token, characters are judged negatively in the degree to which they dislike or misread Shakespeare— as Richard Dalloway does the sonnets, "because it was like listening at keyholes (besides, the relationship was not one that he approved)" (*MD,* p. 84). Similarly, in

Septimus's room, the crass Dr. Holmes "opened Shakespeare—*Antony and Cleopatra;* pushed Shakespeare aside" (*MD,* p. 101); and the imperious Lady Bruton "never spoke of England, but this isle of men, this dear, dear land, was in her blood (without reading Shakespeare)" (*MD,* p. 198).[7]

Clarissa's repeated quotation of the dirge from *Cymbeline*—"Fear no more the heat of the sun"—has generally been taken as her self-encouragement to face life and the demands of the social world, in contrast to Septimus's escape from his fear of life in suicide. It will be recalled, however, that the dirge contains a biting ambiguity, which makes its way into the fiction: the singers are congratulating the supposed departed for escaping the rigors of nature, history, age—of life itself.[8] Thus, Clarissa's affinity for the refrain may be taken as a mark of her own strong propensity for death, in which she imaginatively indulges as she recalls it on her morning walk (*MD,* p. 12), during her mid-day activities (*MD,* p. 45), and at her withdrawal from the party (*MD,* p. 204). A passage from the manuscript of *Mrs. Dalloway* (in the British Museum) makes her drift toward death even clearer by introducing another line of the dirge: "Thou thy worldly task hast done, Mrs. Dalloway read. Tears unshed, tears deep, salt, still, stood about her for all deaths and sorrows . . ." (MS., II, 128). We can sense from this that Clarissa's tendency toward virginal coldness and withdrawal into chaste isolation is an expression of her reversion toward the security of effortless stasis. In this work, as in the early fictions, Virginia Woolf defines character, adumbrates themes, and introduces a pattern of dual impulse— toward life, toward death—based on her use of literary quotations and other elements of her cultural tradition.

It would be impossible, outside the proportions of a

monograph, to indicate the extent to which *To the Lighthouse* operates in this way. The text is rife with quotations and allusions that demand full attention if the fiction's total meaning is to be approached.[9] But one example may serve to illustrate. Browsing through a poetry anthology (in which she also finds Browne's "Syrens' Song"), the heroine, Mrs. Ramsay, turns to Shakespeare's "Sonnet 98." After quoting the mellifluous tenth line (*TL,* p. 186) to her somewhat contemptuous husband (p. 187; he had previously denigrated Shakespeare, largely due to anxieties about his own immortality: *TL,* pp. 70–71), she moves on to the couplet (which is rendered clearer by fuller citation):

They [lily and rose] were but sweet, but figures of de-
   light,
Drawn after you, you pattern of all those.
   Yet seem'd it winter still, and, you away,
   As with your shadow I with these did play.

These lines ultimately derive from the Neoplatonic *topos* of the natural object as a "shadow" of the ideal and ultimately real being. This *topos,* in its Shakespearian presentation, is also related to some of the themes with which *To the Lighthouse* is occupied: the beloved, as having an aesthetic "pattern," of which other lovely objects, like flowers, are mere "figures" (patterned after the pattern); the correlation of winter with the absence of the beloved (this stage of the year being seen as one of death and negation, although implying the cyclical possibility of renewal); and, finally, the "play" of artistic imagination on visible objects in the absence of the beloved whom they embody. This playing with visible substitutes becomes a form of aesthetic recapture of the beloved, reaching toward his or her "shadow"—whether successfully recalling the living spirit is not clear. The shadowy ambiguity of all symbolism—a compound of presence and absence, of substitution and identity—is implicated here and lies near the heart of this great symbolic fiction.

This Shakespearian crux comes toward the close of part one. From that point on, the image of the shadow becomes a constant but ambiguous presence: "For the shadow, the thing folding them in was beginning, [Mrs. Ramsay] felt, to close round her again" (*TL,* pp. 188–189); "she could feel [Ramsay's] mind like a raised hand shadowing her mind" (*TL,* p. 189). In the empty house of part two, "only the shadows of the trees, flourishing in the wind, made obeisance on the wall, and for a moment darkened the pool . . ." (*TL,* pp. 200–201); "among passing shadows and flights of small rain [the spring] seemed to have taken upon her a knowledge of the sorrows of mankind" (*TL,* p. 205). The connections of the shadow are first with troubled interpersonal relations, then with the degeneration of the empty house, and finally with the ephemerality of the seasons and the weight of human cares. The final appearance of the shadow comes as an archetypal figure of death (even more specifically, it is connected with the Hades figure in the fiction's underlying myth of Demeter and Persephone): Lily's climactic vision of the dead Mrs. Ramsay shows her "putting her wreath to her forehead and going unquestioningly with her companion, a shadow, across the fields" (*TL,* p. 279). From these far-flung appearances of the symbol, a pattern of meaning is established, which does not merely reverberate from the initiating quotation but carries the full force of its traditional associations into the drama and into the linguistic substance of the fiction.

The most obviously literary artifice in the Woolf canon is *Orlando: A Biography*. *Orlando* is not merely an infusion of what Harold Nicolson called "the literary element" into the biographical style, but a genuine fusion of two modes of portraying human personality. Fact and imagination are each allowed to contribute to a composite vision of an individual identity, which is itself seen as a composite of its own and others' experience. (Identity is also a fusion of both sexes, and after the hero's sudden sex-change he is referred to as a woman, though really a composite personality.)

Fiction and biography are mixed here by the incorporation of literary texts, from passing allusions to lengthy quotations, into the fabric of the work. A number of scholars have shown that some of the verses the hero, Orlando, composes are taken from the writings of the Sackville family, whose historical line he synthesizes. The quotations range from the Renaissance Thomas Sackville's *Induction* to *The Mirror for Magistrates* (quoted in the manuscript but replaced by intentionally trivial lines in the published text) to passages from Vita Sackville-West's set of Georgics, *The Land* —which is the original of Orlando's poem, "The Oak Tree." [10] The inclusion in a biography of a writer's own prose or poetry is by no means unusual, but it is attended in *Orlando* by a firm principle for such inclusions: "biographers and critics might save themselves all their labours if readers would only take this advice. For when we read: [five lines of *The Rape of the Lock* quoted]—we know as if we heard him how Mr. Pope's tongue flickered like a lizard's, how his eyes flashed, how his hand trembled, how he loved, how he lied, how he suffered. In short, every secret of a writer's soul, every experience of his life, every quality of his mind is written large in his works . . ." (*O,* pp. 189–190). We

have here an extension of the style-is-the-man cliché
to biography; for, if the style reveals the man's traits
and even inner experience, it is enough to incorporate
parts of his work to give sufficient indication of his mind
and soul.

Given this equation—subsequently qualified—of the
writer and his work, Woolf does go on to quote entire
paragraphs of Addison and of Swift; and in each case
her persona, the biographer of Orlando, claims to "hold
that gentleman, cocked hat and all, in the hollow of
our hands" (*O,* p. 190). Elsewhere, Woolf attempts to
describe the mind of her biographical subject by directly
or indirectly citing his reading and theater-going experiences. Orlando not only observes Shakespeare in the
act of composition (*O,* pp. 22–23), but sees a street
performance of *Othello,* bringing three lines of the
postmurder speech into the fabric of the fiction (*O,* p.
54; from act 5, scene 2, lines 99–101). Sir Thomas
Browne's prose is, on the other hand, not directly
quoted, but its effects are richly described: "Like an
incantation rising from all parts of the room, from the
night wind and the moonlight, rolled the divine melody
of those words which, lest they should outstare this
page, we will leave where they lie entombed, not dead,
embalmed rather, so fresh is their colour, so sound their
breathing . . ." (*O,* p. 76; Browne is also mentioned on
pp. 68 and 69, as part of the bout of reading that further inspires Orlando in his artistic vocation).

Beyond these direct quotations and detailed descriptions of literary experience, there are numerous evoca-
tions of the history of English literature. Through the
perennial poetaster, Nick Greene, Orlando learns the
gossip about the Renaissance poets (*O,* pp. 82–85);
she becomes a patroness of Pope and his circle and sees
the shadows of Johnson and Boswell (*O,* p. 201); she

marries a man who has Shelley's entire works by heart
(*O,* p. 235) and writes a mawkish kind of Romantic
verse herself (before a spilled inkpot blots it out: *O,*
p. 215) ; her imagination is stocked with scenes from
the Victorian classics, like the passing of Arthur from
Tennyson's *Idylls of the King* (*O,* p. 223) and the
climactic duel in Thackeray's *Henry Esmond* (*O,* p.
256; this scene may, however, be derived from Orlando's personal experience in the eighteenth century).
The narrative voice, as well, adds touches of parody to
fill in the medium of literature in which the heroine
has her being: "let other pens treat of sex and sexuality;
we quit such odious subjects as soon as we can" concludes the account of Orlando's sex change (*O,* p. 128;
a parody of the first sentence of the last chapter of
Mansfield Park). And the parodic constitution of the
heroine catches up the literary sensation of the moment,
as Orlando is compared with the recently arrived Lady
Chatterly: "Surely, since she is a woman, and a beautiful woman, and a woman in the prime of life, she will
soon give over this pretence of writing and thinking
and begin at least to think of a gamekeeper. . . . all of
which is, of course, the very stuff of life and the only
possible subject for fiction" (*O,* p. 242).

These remarks and a host of others like them are
important less as criticism than as an aesthetic mode:
they help to build up a literary atmosphere, a world
of words, in which the subject of this biography moves.
Orlando is a literary biography, not merely in recount-
ing the formation and milieu of a writer, Vita Sackville-West, but in transforming that account into literature itself—making her biography a literary object,
which is her adequate symbol. This fiction is made out
of literature in somewhat the same way that Vita
Sackville-West's sensibility as a writer was made up of

her own and her ancestor's literary experiences. In this way, *Orlando* becomes—along with *Ulysses* and, as we shall see, *Between the Acts*—a prime instance of the encyclopedic style fashioning an entire work of art.

"Of course, there's the whole of English literature to choose from. But how can one choose?" (*BA*, p. 73). Mrs. Swithin expresses the problem of *Between the Acts* in her usual vague way; the discussion is of choosing a play for amateur theatricals, but she turns it to the subject of her own reading habits. As early as the opening scene, in which Bart Oliver remembers his mother's gift of the works of Byron—and quotes from two of the more famous lyrics—the characters of *Between the Acts* are as self-conscious as their creator about the presence of English literature in their midst.

At times this is a merely formal presence, as when Isa Oliver runs her eyes over the books of the Pointz Hall Library, ranging from *The Faerie Queen* to *The Antiquities of Durham,* before settling down to a newspaper account of a rape committed by the venerable Horse Guards. Alternatively, there is an effort to bring literature to bear upon the self and its concerns: " 'I fear I am not in my perfect mind,' Giles [Oliver] muttered. . . . Words came to the surface—he remembered 'a stricken deer in whose lean flank the world's harsh scorn has struck its thorn . . .' " (*BA,* pp. 103–104)—mingling lines from *King Lear* (act 4, scene 7, line 63) and Cowper's *The Task* (book III, line 108; the rhyming phrases are Giles's invention). More often, the nation's literary endowment furnishes catch phrases imperfectly recalled—"Books: the treasured life-blood of immortal spirits. Poets: the legislators of mankind" (*BA,* p. 138) —mellifluous lines to be mindlessly chanted, like Bart's repetition of the opening lines of Swinburne's

"Itylus" (*BA,* pp. 137, 139, etc.), and vaguely expressive sentiments: "did you feel when the shower fell, someone wept for us all? There's a poem, *Tears tears tears,* it begins. And goes on *O then the unloosened ocean* . . . but I can't remember the rest" (*BA,* p. 234; the lines are from one of the poems of Whitman's "Sea Drift").

The composition of the pageant that is enacted in the fiction is not different in kind from the characters' mouthings, incorporating as it does the fragments of English literature that lie scattered about in modern culture. It can stand as a gently satirical instance of the doctrines of Eliot, Pound, and others on the unconscious incorporation of tradition in the individual artist's talent. The conventions of Elizabethan stagecraft and rhetoric are imitated—even specific lines quoted, for example, *"Play out the play"* (*BA,* p. 107; from *I Henry IV,* act 2, scene 4, line 531). Not only plots, characters, and verbal formulas are taken up, but also the classical *topoi* of the genre most appropriate to a pageant, the masque: *"Time, leaning on his sickle, stands amazed. While commerce from her Cornucopia pours the mingled tribute of her different ores"* (*BA,* p. 147). Similarly, the longest and best written of the literary parodies that make up the pageant, *Where There's a Will There's a Way,* is an imitation of Restoration comic tropes. And the satire of the shibboleths of Victorianism is largely a parody of literature become cliché, like the descent of Moore's "The Last Rose of Summer" to the level of a popular song (*BA,* p. 198), or the use of Kipling's "The White Man's Burden" as a jingoist catch phrase (*BA,* p. 191).

The pageant's synthesis of English literature reaches a climax when the characters reappear for a finale and mingle their representative ages by dancing together in their varied costumes. The impression of a unity of historical experience is enforced by their medley of fragmentary phrases from their parts:

> *I am not* (said one) *in my perfect mind* [*Lear*, cf. *BA*, p. 103] . . . Another, *Reason am I . . . Home is the hunter, home from the hill* [approximating Stevenson's "Requiem"] . . . *Home? Where the miner sweats, and the maiden faith is rudely strumpeted* [Shakespeare's "Sonnet 66"; "faith" is substituted for "virtue"] . . . *Sweet and low; sweet and low, wind of the western sea* [Tennyson's *The Princess*] . . . *Is that a dagger that I see before me?* [approximately *Macbeth*, act 2, scene 1, line 33] . . . *I'd be a butterfly. I'd be a butterfly* [song by Thomas Haynes Bayly, sung on p. 188] . . . *In thy will is our peace* [*Paradiso*, canto III, line 85] . . . *Hark, hark, the dogs do bark and the beggars . . . .* [nursery rhyme] (*BA*, pp. 215–216)[11]

Out of these snippets of literature—juxtaposing the loftiest and the most banal strains, the universal and the homely, the sentimental and the sardonic—is made the substance of the pageant. This crescendo of words suggests that the pageant is not a mere pastiche of English literature but a representation of the collective mind of England, which is composed of just such bits and pieces of language.

What is true for the pageant is true for *Between the Acts* itself, in the frame story that is interwoven with the play. At a number of points, the narrative catches up lines of poetry and prose and makes them an effective part of its texture, as in the final scene of the Olivers' reunion, when "Heart of Darkness" is evoked to describe their fate of love and conflict. Elsewhere the mode of incorporation is more elaborate, as when

E. M. Forster's *A Passage to India* is imitated: "Beyond that [cloud] was blue, pure blue, black blue: blue that had never filtered down; that had escaped registration" (*BA,* p. 30; part of the penultimate paragraph of Forster's first chapter reads: "Clouds map [the sky] up at times, but it is normally a dome of blending tints, and the main tint blue. By day the blue will pale down. . . . But the core of blue persists, and so it is by night. . . . that farther distance, though beyond cloud, last freed itself from blue."). Or the allusion may be so subtle as to defy decisive attribution, as in an echoing of Gertrude Stein's most famous line, Mrs. Swithin "left the sentence unfinished, as if she were of two minds, and they fluttered to right and to left, like pigeons rising from the grass" (*BA,* p. 91). Although she is not to be taken as a definitive spokesman, when Mrs. Swithin shows William Dodge over the house she indicates the theme progressively established in the text: "Then she ran her hand over the sunk books in the wall on the landing, as if they were pan pipes. 'Here are the poets from whom we descend by way of the mind . . .' " (*BA,* pp. 84–85).

It thus becomes clear that an important strain in Woolf's experimentalism was akin to that of her greatest contemporaries: the use of the past—especially the literature of the past—either for the purposes of ironic commentary on the present, or as providing organizing *mythoi* to deal with modern experience, or as a fund of communal culture to which the solitary mind can relate itself. If *Orlando* and *Between the Acts* may be said to derive from the same literary impulses that move *The Waste Land* and the *Cantos, The Voyage Out* and *Night and Day* will be found to anticipate them in the way that "Prufrock" and "Mauberly" prefigure their creators' later work. Virginia Woolf is to be seen as an artist fully at one with the modern movement of experimentation and innovation, but, as is the case with the other major figures of the period, her novelty is most often a variation on traditional themes, her discovery is characteristically an insight into truths of long standing in our culture.

Notes

1. Virginia Woolf, *A Writer's Diary,* ed. Leonard Woolf (London: Hogarth Press, 1965 [1953]), p. 80; 27 June 1925.

2. Virginia Woolf, *The Voyage Out* (London: Hogarth Press, 1965), p. 33. This, the Hogarth Press Uniform Edition, will be cited throughout my text by abbreviated title and page numbers as follows:

VO: The Voyage Out.
ND: Night and Day.
MD: Mrs. Dalloway.
TL: To the Lighthouse.
O: Orlando.
BA: Between the Acts.

3. R. C. Jebb, trans. and ed., *Sophocles: The Plays and Fragments* (Cambridge: at the University Press, 1888), III, 69–71. For Woolf's persistent return to the image of Antigone, see Jean Guiguet, *Virginia Woolf and Her Works,* trans. Jean Stewart (London: Hogarth Press, 1965), pp. 419 and 464.

4. Harvena Richter also comments on this irony in *Virginia Woolf: The Inward Voyage* (Princeton: Princeton University Press, 1970), pp. 124–125.

5. Others have perceived the novel's relation to Shakespeare: Josephine O. Schaefer, *The Three-Fold Nature of Reality in the Novels of Virginia Woolf* (The Hague: Mouton, 1965), p. 50, points to the affinity of its action with that of *Twelfth Night;* and Jean O. Love, *Worlds in Consciousness: Mytho-*

poetic Thought in the Novels of Virginia Woolf (Berkeley, Los Angeles, and London: University of California Press, 1970), p. 118, remarks on Mrs. Hilbery's place in the tradition of the "wise fool."

6. Her theory of Anne Hathaway's authorship of the sonnets leads Quentin Bell to name Woolf's aunt, Anne Ritchie, as Mrs. Hilbery's prototype (*Virginia Woolf: A Biography* [London: Hogarth Press, 1972], I, 11 n).

7. Given this presence of Shakespeare, it comes as no surprise that Mrs. Hilbery not only appears in *Mrs. Dalloway* at a crucial point, toward the end of the climactic party (pp. 209–210), but is also endowed with some of the mana ascribed to her in *Night and Day:* "And up came that wandering will-o'-the-wisp, that vagous phosphorescence, old Mrs. Hilbery . . ." (*MD,* p. 193; Mrs. Hilbery is also mentioned on p. 135).

8. For additional implications of the quotation, see Maud Bodkin, *Archetypal Patterns in Poetry: Psychological Studies of Imagination* (London: Oxford University Press, 1963), pp. 87–88.

9. To my knowledge, only Ruby Cohn, "Art in *To the Lighthouse,*" *Modern Fiction Studies* 8 (1962–1963): 127–136, takes the trouble to examine a number of these allusions. Another contribution to our knowledge of these works is Jean M. Wyatt, "*Mrs. Dalloway:* Literary Allusion as Structural Metaphor," *PMLA* 88 (1973): 440–451.

10. For the unpublished quote, see Charles G. Hoffman, "Fact and Fantasy in *Orlando:* Virginia Woolf's Manuscript Revisions," *Texas Studies in Literature and Language* 10 (1968): 442; for the published quotes and other relationships, see Frank Baldanza, "*Orlando* and the Sackvilles," *PMLA* 70 (1955): 274–279. Other family poems that Woolf thought of quoting are the lyrics of the Restoration poet, Charles Sackville, Earl of Dorset; the manuscript (which is now at the Sackville estate at Knole) contains stanzas from his "Song" ("May knaves and fools grow rich and great") and "On the Countess of Dorchester" ("Tell me, Dorinda, why so gay . . .").

11. The broken-off line ends "are coming to town"; it is also quoted on p. 139. This is no. 410 in *The Oxford Dictionary of Nursery Rhymes;* another entry, "Sing a Song of Six-

pence" (no. 486), is used as a verbal equivalent of a musical refrain in the pageant, on pp. 137, 146, 211, and 212; it is also imitated by Isa on p. 208. Folk art here plays much the same role as "high" art in constituting the pageant's evocation of a group mind or culture.

SEVEN

Fiction at the Edge of Poetry: Durrell, Beckett, Green

John Unterecker

THE works of Lawrence Durrell, Samuel Beckett, and Henry Green are examples of certain twentieth-century ways of approaching reality—ways that significantly differ from earlier ways and that consequently force the work of these writers out of conventional novelistic patterns.

In some respects most of what I want to say has already been said. Mr. Fleishman, talking of Virginia Woolf's unhappiness with the word *novel,* and Hillis Miller, showing how patterns of repetition dominate and help explain the structure of a work, anticipated much of what I want to talk about. Like Charles Rossman, who helped illuminate the relationship between art and life in Joyce, I am also concerned with the interrelationship between art and life. And though I will be devoting relatively little time to those problems of dualism Mr. Cowan investigated, problems of dualism crop up in almost everything I want to consider. Finally, while I expect to evade matters of ethics, all three of the novelists I deal with are deeply concerned with ethical problems—though never in quite the same way John Galsworthy was.

Let me briefly outline what I hope to demonstrate. First of all, I want to suggest ways in which these three novelists—Durrell, Beckett, and Green—parallel a number of other novelists and poets, particularly Joyce and the poets James Wright and Wallace Stevens and (in a short digression) John Keats.

I want to begin with a James Wright poem that sets a scene, that presents a moment fully, and that then makes an oblique commentary on that scene. In other words, I want to offer an example of a poem that stops time long enough to discover an enormous emotional response to a frozen moment. "Time" in such a poem is like a shutter snapping. Its design is *image: statement of feeling.* But feeling in poetry of this sort is always larger than image and almost always oblique to it.

I then want to go on to examine one way in which reality is apprehended in much modern fiction, to suggest that it is a very complex way of apprehension, that it centers on the present moment, that because of this peculiarly twentieth-century focus terms like *objective* and *subjective* become relatively meaningless and such literary techniques as naturalism and symbolism lose much of their force. In the process, I wish to imply that much of our fiction takes on the quality either of a poem like the Wright poem that I am about to quote or, setting the snapshot in motion, a cinematic quality. Though other works might be more familiar, I shall draw examples of what I'm talking about from Henry Green's *Pack My Bag* and *Loving,* from Lawrence

Durrell's *Tunc* and *Nunquam,* and from Samuel Beckett's *How It Is.*

This is James Wright's poem: an image followed by an oblique commentary. The poem's entire action is confined to a single step across a barbed wire fence. It represents one way—a poet's way—of dealing with reality. If it can be held in mind through what follows, it may make some of the parallel action of one kind of poetry and one kind of fiction clearer.

A BLESSING

Just off the highway to Rochester, Minnesota,
Twilight bounds softly forth on the grass.
And the eyes of those two Indian ponies
Darken with kindness.
They have come gladly out of the willows
To welcome my friend and me.
We step over the barbed wire into the pasture
Where they have been grazing all day, alone.
They ripple tensely, they can hardly contain their
    happiness
That we have come.
They bow shyly as wet swans. They love each other.
There is no loneliness like theirs.
At home once more,
They begin munching the young tufts of spring in the
    darkness.
I would like to hold the slenderer one in my arms,
For she has walked over to me
And nuzzled my left hand.
She is black and white,
Her mane falls wild on her forehead,
And the light breeze moves me to caress her long ear
That is delicate as the skin over a girl's wrist.

Suddenly I realize
That if I stepped out of my body I would break
Into blossom.[1]

Now let me turn to my subject matter—a vast one,
perhaps half of contemporary fiction. To give my paper
the illusion of coherence, I've arbitrarily selected my
three landmark figures. I see them as something like
standing stones on an enormous field. But they are
arbitrarily chosen: any of dozens of other figures could
have served as well. I've selected these three only
because I am most fond of, most familiar with their
work.

Their work does conveniently illustrate, however,
some of the ways in which contemporary fiction is
moving away from the various kinds of well-made
novels that the nineteenth and early twentieth centuries
had invented. As I've already mentioned, critical terms
that until the mid-twenties of this century were enormously valuable—terms like *realistic, naturalistic,* even
symbolist—no longer seem even faintly applicable to
the most interesting contemporary works. They seem
no longer applicable, I feel, because the very realities
that realists, naturalists, and symbolists had attempted
to define have for all practical purposes evaporated.
Neither life nor the spiritual life is quite like that—
quite so simple as that—anymore.

What is really interesting about the nineteenth and
early twentieth centuries is how completely people of
those periods took reality for granted. There seemed
for most thinking men of those times to be little or no
question about the nature of reality: it was everything
"out there." The big questions about reality were how
it got that way (the problem the naturalists tackled
head-on) and whether there was some sort of super-

reality of the mind or soul (the problem the symbolists took on).

The grandest intellectual pursuits of the nineteenth century were almost all in these areas: *how?* and *what more?* On the one hand, there was Darwin trying to calculate how all of the inhabitant plants and animals of the world had evolved to their present state, Freud trying to account for the adult by laborious recovery of childhood and earliest infancy, and the followers of Newton working out a physics that would account for experiential reality—all of them assuming an incontrovertible present reality and all searching for causes that would adequately explain it. And on the other hand, there were the opium eaters, the mesmerists, the spiritualists, and the ecstatic visionaries—almost all looking for some kind of a superreality different from, superior to, and in a sense also causative of day-to-day reality. But reality itself was unquestioned. It was there: solid, obvious, as real as a standing stone in a field.

Reality is a good deal harder to pin down now than in earlier generations—largely because we have noticed that, the closer we get to it, the harder it is to see. Perhaps, indeed, our most important twentieth-century observation has been that, as the mode of apprehending reality changes, reality itself undergoes significant changes. What there is depends almost entirely on how we see.

Now this, of course, is no great news. We have all become adjusted to the Heisenberg principle, and those of us who are not in the sciences have nevertheless learned in a very secondhand way a little bit about the machinery of quantum physics. What I do think is worth asserting, however, is that something rather like the principle of indeterminacy seems to have become quite casually accepted by many of our most interesting novelists. Except perhaps for Durrell, who deliberately set out in *The Alexandria Quartet* to illustrate the notion that the observer alters the thing observed, most of these novelists are hardly interested in adapting scientific theory to a technique of fiction. Yet, in writer after writer, we find reality changing as the focus of observation changes.

Since, from here on, the word *focus* is going to be an obsessive image, I should pause to explain that it seems to me likely that the rather insubstantial reality that Durrell, Green, and Beckett present is at least in part a consequence of their having learned to see with camera eyes. That is, rather than dealing with an evasive reality in a scientific or philosophical format, they find themselves presenting reality as if it were seen through a lens. Now this way of looking is really vastly different from that of most earlier novelists. One has only to compare the presentational techniques of, say, Henry James—who, after all, was familiar with the camera but who had learned to see long before the motion picture began to dominate our way of looking at things—with, for example, Joyce, who was fascinated with framed images, though he, too, did much of his writing before the motion pictures had made much headway.

James almost always builds scenes theatrically. With very little effort, one can divide his novels into acts and scenes—long scenes that work out a human problem in an arena that looks remarkably like a stage set. And we, as audience, have about as much mobility as people sitting in a theater: everything is always spread out there in front of us, exactly just so many feet away, and the whole panorama is almost constantly available to us. The relationship between us and the reality on that stage is a fixed one. Joyce, on the other hand, seems

to me characteristically to engage in a steadily shifting
focus. Joyce's novel is the lens between us and the
action, so that the action itself is pulled toward us,
moved off to a long shot, held in a medium frame,
brought in again. Distance—or at least apparent distance—is constantly changing. Consider, for example,
the last few lines of *The Dead.* Gabriel Conroy is
standing by the window of a hotel bedroom. His wife,
Gretta, has fallen asleep, exhausted from the party she
and her husband have just come back from and exhausted also by the tale she has told of the dead boy
Michael Furey, whom she loved once and who had died
of love for her. Standing alone by the window, Gabriel,
for an instant, seems to be in some sort of communion
with the dead:

> His soul had approached that region where dwell the
> vast hosts of the dead. He was conscious of, but could
> not apprehend, their wayward and flickering exis-
> tence. His own identity was fading out into a grey
> impalpable world: the solid world itself which
> these dead had one time reared and lived in was
> dissolving and dwindling.
>
> A few light taps upon the pane made him turn
> to the window. It had begun to snow again. He
> watched sleepily the flakes, silver and dark, falling
> obliquely against the lamplight. The time had come
> for him to set out on his journey westward. Yes, the
> newspapers were right: snow was general all over
> Ireland. It was falling on every part of the dark
> central plain, on the treeless hills, falling softly upon
> the Bog of Allen and, farther westward, softly falling
> into the dark mutinous Shannon waves. It was falling,
> too, upon every part of the lonely churchyard on
> the hill where Michael Furey lay buried. It lay thickly

drifted on the crooked crosses and headstones, on
the spears of the little gate, on the barren thorns.
His soul swooned slowly as he heard the snow falling
faintly through the universe and faintly falling, like
the descent of their last end, upon all the living and
the dead.

Joyce's handling of this scene is, I believe, essentially
cinematic. As the solid world dissolves and dwindles,
his focus is on the snowflakes on the window pane.
Then, abruptly, we are lifted to a vision of snow "general all over Ireland": snow on "every part of the dark
central plain," snow "on the treeless hills," snow
"falling softly upon the Bog of Allen and, farther west-
ward, softly falling into the dark mutinous Shannon
waves." But then Joyce's focus moves sharply in on a
particular scene: "It was falling, too, upon every part
of the lonely churchyard on the hill where Michael
Furey lay buried." And again his focus moves in, aban-
doning the panorama of the churchyard for details
within it: the snow "lay thickly drifted on the crooked
crosses and headstones." And once again the focus cuts
in, blocking out all other detail, to the "spears of the
little gate," and finally in extreme, almost microscopic,
close-up to the "barren thorns" themselves. Only then
can that focus widen. But, when it does widen, its scope
becomes enormous. For now it encompasses all things:
"the snow falling faintly through the universe and
faintly falling, like the descent of their last end, upon
all the living and the dead."

I do not want, of course, to suggest for a minute that
this kind of observation is limited only to the twentieth
century. We can find it occasionally in almost all writers.
Eyes themselves do, after all, operate through shifting
focuses. We find, for example, at the end of "The Eve

of St. Agnes" a treatment of focus that is almost precisely parallel to that which Joyce uses in *The Dead.*
Keats, you remember, has Porphyro and Madeline
awake from their love sleep to a predawn snowstorm
not altogether unlike that Gabriel watches. The lovers
make their way out of Madeline's chamber and begin
an extraordinarily cinematic descent down the stairs
and out the castle door:

> Down the wide stairs a darkling way they found—
> In all the house was heard no human sound.

Like Joyce, Keats also focuses in more and more closely
on details of the scene: lamps, tapestries, an "iron
porch" where a drunken porter lies asleep, a bloodhound who rises and shakes himself. And as Joyce was
later to do, Keats also toward the end narrows the focus
down more and more precisely: first to the bolts on
the castle door, then to the chains beside it, and, finally,
to the key turning in the lock. And then at the very
end, he also, like Joyce, abruptly widens the focus from
the particular details of the castle door to the vast storm
of all time that the lovers enter. The pattern is view-
of-the-scene, detail, more minute detail, most minute
detail, and then an enormous panorama that takes in
not only unlimited space but unlimited time as well:

> Down the wide stairs a darkling way they found—
> In all the house was heard no human sound.
> A chain-drooped lamp was flickering by each door;
> The arras, rich with horseman, hawk, and hound,
> Flutter'd in the besieging wind's uproar;
> And the long carpets rose along the gusty floor.
>
> They glide, like phantoms, into the wide hall;
> Like phantoms, to the iron porch they glide,
> Where lay the Porter, in uneasy sprawl,

With a huge empty flagon by his side:
The wakeful bloodhound rose, and shook his hide,
But his sagacious eye an inmate owns;
By one, and one, the bolts full easy slide:——
The chains lie silent on the footworn stones;——
The key turns, and the door upon its hinges groans.

And they are gone: ay, ages long ago
The lovers fled away into the storm.

One can, as I have said, find examples of this sort
of following, shifting focus in any number of writers
from any number of centuries; but it is not until recent
times that it begins in any significant way to affect
the form of fiction itself. Yet in writers as unlike each
other as Robbe-Grillet and William Burroughs, to take
two conspicuous examples, cinematic observation
almost completely determines form.

In other contemporary writers, as in the three this
paper will touch on, cinematic observation becomes a
technique through which the complexity of reality can
be presented. For unlike the writers of earlier times,
who wanted to explain how reality got to be the way it
is, Durrell, Green, and Beckett are really far more
interested in the mysterious thing itself: the real nature
of what in fact *is* out there. And their techniques of
apprehending reality can be much more immediately
grasped in terms of long-shot, close-up, panning, and
zooming-in than in terms either of heredity and environment or of symbolic action. Nineteenth-century
approaches are not eliminated; they are simply by-
passed or understressed. The focus changes, and the
world changes with it.

Consider, as a first example, several passages from
Henry Green. Though I will soon touch on his fiction,

here I want to take a few lines from the opening pages of *Pack My Bag,* an autobiographical account of his formative years. He is trying to explain something that seems to him important about the limits of memory and the consequent difficulty of dealing with a lost past: "Most people remember very little of when they were small," he says, "and what small part of this time there is that stays is coloured and readjusted until the picture which was there, what does come back, has been over-painted and retouched enough to make it an unreliable account of what used to be. But while the presentation is inaccurate and so can no longer be called a movie, or a set of stills, it does gain by what it is not, or, in other words, it does set out what seems to have gone on; that is it gives, as far as such things can and as far as they can be interesting, what one thinks has gone to make one up." [2]

Now the important thing here is not just that Green uses imagery of movies and stills but that his concern is with the limits that are necessarily imposed on us in any effort to recover the reality of the past—a past that is "unreliable" because it is "coloured," "readjusted," "over-painted," "retouched," that is "inaccurate" because it has become "what it is not"; for it has become an illusion seen through the soft-focus lenses of memory, "what one thinks has gone to make one up," a thing not of vision but of revision, a thing, finally, of pure *seeming,* "what seems to have gone on."

Or consider another example from *Pack My Bag*— again an example that draws on motion-picture imagery but that is more essentially concerned with the way in which reality is apprehended. Green is talking about his life at Oxford: "Those were the days of silent films," he says,

when anyone with a hangover wept at words of his
own he put onto the lips of the girl reproving her
drunken lover on the screen, of Mary Pickford, "The
World's Sweetheart," speechless yet or, for girls, of
Valentino who never said a word in films. For me
the darkness, that is the light subdued, the snivelling
and soft laughs, those heads more intent on each
other's breath as in the oldest gesture they inclined
one to the other against the lighted screen the orchestra played low to, here was the place in which to
work out the sense of guilt, to conquer that nausea
of lunch after the night before's drinking. The days
were a stupor until, in the evening with a few quick
drinks, the mind was lit again by the daylight of
whiskey with friends, and after more hock, because
we mixed our drinks, the old kaleidoscope reappeared
of the fabulous relationships between people known
to all of us with the spotlight of confidences; all this
when Rome was perhaps already burning.[3]

The passage is interesting for a number of reasons.
For one thing, it seems to move too quickly; we glide
in a parenthetical phrase from silent movies to a
drinking bout. Yet the apparently irrational transition
has a rationale of its own, skidding along, as it does,
on an imagery greased with light. The lovers who
project the words they want to hear into the mouths of
Mary Pickford and Valentino are at first pictured in
"the darkness," but darkness is instantly redefined as
"the light subdued," and soon we see the lovers' heads
in silhouette "against the lighted screen the orchestra
played low to." Evenings lighted up with whisky and
hock rather than with film and projector now take over,
for under the control of alcohol the audience itself
becomes equated to the figures on the screen. Private

individuals are now the "fabulous" ones—as fabulous
as Pickford and Valentino, their confidences the "spotlight" that picks out otherwise dark "relationships."
Each separate evening mind is "*lit again* by the *daylight*
of whisky with friends" (my italics) as their intricate
rapport becomes a thing of colored, mirrored light,
"the old kaleidoscope . . . of the fabulous relationships
between people known to all of us with the spotlight
of confidences." Here we are offered layers of realities:
the fiction on the silent screen; the secondary fiction we
create by putting private dialogue into the mouths of
the fabulous creatures on the screen; the tertiary fiction
we participate in when under alcohol we move into
the spotlighted arena that the camera observes, when
we ourselves become fabulous creatures—and, outside
and beyond all of these fictions, the real world in which
Rome, perhaps, burns, the old-fashioned external reality
of fact: Europe caught in the days just prior to World
War II. Yet for every *fiction* I have just listed, we can
substitute the word *reality;* for every *reality* we can
substitute the word *fiction.* Point of view determines
reality, and truth is nothing more and nothing less than
the angle of observation of a distorting observer, truth
nothing more and nothing less than a distorting observer's relationship to a distorted thing imperfectly
observed. As Durrell points out, the new physics "is
founded upon the theory that we cannot observe the
course of nature without disturbing it"; and the consequence for the writer is that he can "no longer objec-
tivize" the world.[4] Reality is no longer "out there"; it
is entangled in the subjectivity of every observer.

What happens when this kind of a point of view
intrudes on the novel is extraordinarily like what
happens inside many poems. "Life's nonsense pierces
us," Wallace Stevens says, "with strange relation." The

passage comes from "Notes toward a Supreme Fiction."
The "supreme fiction," of course, is the work of art,
specifically the poem, explicitly the particular poem
that is in the process of being constructed. The "strange
relation" Stevens deals with is that of varyingly observed
reality, a reality compounded from "nonsense"—mere
being—but nonsense that under the artist's focusing
eye makes sense of a kind—as, for example, the daytime
call of a wood-dove, the nighttime incantation of an
astrologer, and the uninterrupted day-and-night roar
of the sea—all shouting "hoo" and all met together
only in the accident of Stevens's ear noticing their
common call and, within his poem, calling that call
to our attention:

> We say: At night an Arabian in my room,
> With his damned hoobla-hoobla-hoobla-how,
> Inscribes a primitive astronomy
>
> Across the unscrawled fores the future casts
> And throws his stars around the floor. By day
> The wood-dove used to chant his hoobla-hoo
>
> And still the grossest irridescence of ocean
> Howls hoo and rises and howls hoo and falls.
> Life's nonsense pierces us with strange relation.[5]

Reality, in such a structure, becomes not what is "out
there" but instead what seems, to go back to Henry
Green, to cohere. Reality becomes the illusion of coherence. In terms of many poems and in terms of a number
of contemporary novels, reality of this sort can best
be diagrammed as a tissue of verbal interrelationships:
life's nonsense piercing us with strange relation. What
really communicates in such a structure is not statements of fact but rather inferences about states of being,
"feelings" of "relatedness." In the Stevens poem, for

example, ostensibly unrelated but overlapping images are presented and then a statement is made that does not so much give them meaning as itself seem meaningful because of them.

One last passage from *Pack My Bag* before we turn to some works of fiction. Green is here trying to justify his decision to eliminate from his autobiography the names of all individuals he had known and most places he had been. In the process, he feels compelled to defend a kind of prose that might just as well be called poetry: "Prose should be a long intimacy between strangers with no direct appeal to what both may have known. It should slowly appeal to feelings unexpressed, it should in the end draw tears out of the stone, and feelings are not bounded by the associations common to place names or to persons with whom the reader is unexpectedly familiar." [6]

Such prose, prose that represents "a long intimacy between strangers" and that appeals "to feelings un-expressed," does indeed "draw tears out of the stone," for it makes us aware, if we are lucky enough to respond to it, of the nature of what we, here and now, must regard as our own reality—a reality that is neither solipsistic nor objective, but rather a reality that repre-sents *an entanglement of being:* myself, yourself, Henry Green, a crowd of strangers who define each other in our accidental *intimate* interpenetration of sensibilities. Through such interpenetration, the reality we partici-pate in becomes not more *real* than either "objective" or "subjective" reality but instead infinitely richer. Though such a reality can never be apprehended in itself, something of its form, at least, can be suggested when we read reports of what eyes other than our own have seen. We can then begin to sense not its "real" shape—that is forever out of reach—but at least a little of its complex surface geography that our own two eyes cannot make out.

Let me construct an image for what I have in mind. Say we set up a statue in a park. Because women are beautiful, let us make her a woman and, because we are interested in reality, let us leave her unclothed. She stands there, a chunk of most realistically carved marble, so lifelike she might in fact be flesh, a naked woman about, say, to lift her arms to us. (We can already see the muscles tightening under her skin.) If we listen carefully we can imagine that we hear the first sound forming behind her half-parted lips. Certainly, she is about to say "come to me," "kiss me," "call me by name," a phrase of some infinitely intimate sort beginning with the sound of a *k.* There she stands, already as much in love with us as we are with her. But how do we apprehend her reality? We stand in front of her, admiring the way the hazy sunlight models her thighs; we move around her, as if she were indeed any statue in a park, and back again in front—and already she has changed. A cloud has come between us and the sun, and the hazy modulations of her thighs have been replaced by grey marble. Those other glimpses of her that we have had—side, back, other side—are already contaminated by memory, their sharp focus muddied by the reality of what we at the moment see. But we are still in pursuit of bare reality itself; and we move in toward her body—a foot, say, from her foot. Here, alas, her lovely skin takes on the grain of stone. Closer yet, and she is completely gone, nothing at all left of the charmer but flecks of light bouncing off flecks of rock. For we are all—as she is—trapped in space and constantly vanishing backward out of being into nothingness. Change, which we call time, tears all of us to shreds. So we will never comprehend her. There is simply no way for any of us to see her from all sides, all angles, all distances simultaneously. No matter how close to her we come or how widely we circle her—whether we amble or make a pell-mell run, whirling around her like a speeded-up second hand—we can never apprehend her full reality; as each second ticks, she and we change. A drop of rain strikes her marble skin, and an infinitely tiny chip flakes off to wash away forever; as I focus my eyes on her eyes, a synapse uncouples for the last time in my brain and I lose forever a fragment memory of how for an instant she once had been. If a man can never entirely grasp the image of a statue in a park, how infinitely more difficult it must be for anyone to apprehend her reality if, like Galatea, she suddenly takes on a life of flesh and blood. For then change dominates everything. No matter how still she stands, breath lifts her breasts, blood flushes her face and, final complication, she herself becomes a seeing apprehending being, conscious that she is being watched, herself watching, judging, evaluating all those thousands of figures who stalk round and round her, listening to their silences, trying to read some message into their questioning eyes.

How then can we fully experience her being? Never entirely by ourselves. It is here the artist must come in—the stranger with a foreign pair of eyes, the stranger who shares with us for a few pages of words his intimate sense of what it is we are both looking at. We will not—cannot—see the same girl; but we will at least each know what the other has missed.

My lady in the park, the observant reader will already realize, comes kissing close to one that Durrell himself constructed and bears, I hope, an echoing relationship to an ancient male variant that Beckett tossed face down into a sea of mud and *merde*.

I want to take up Durrell's lady first; for anyone
who has read *Tunc* and *Nunquam,* a pair of books that
Durrell himself describes as "a two-part novel of an
old-fashioned sort," [7] is likely either to have become
completely exasperated by or to have fallen in love
with her. Durrell's Galatea is a reconstruction of an
extraordinarily beautiful motion-picture actress,
Iolanthe, who has had, in the first of his two novels,
the very bad grace to die. The other figures in the novel,
however, are not content to let her pass out of the world;
aiding a scientist, they construct an ingeniously com-
puterized plastic likeness of her, into the memory banks
of which has been fed all of her available history except
her death. To make her human, or at least as human
as a machine can be, her computer brain is sufficiently
randomized as to give her the possibility of choice.
What fascinates Durrell, of course, is that, once she
has been set into action, his characters respond to her
as if she were alive. And indeed, for all practical purposes, she is: she remembers, she thinks, she hates, she
loves. Though all of them know about her plastic skin
and electric emotions, they compulsively respond to
her own responses. Some of the book's readers have also
had the same reactions—at least if one can judge by
reviews. They praise her or blame her precisely as if
she were flesh and blood.

Though *Tunc* and *Nunquam* are not really as effective a demonstration of the complex nature of reality
as that massive major work, *The Alexandria Quartet,*
in the single character of Iolanthe the paired novels
do demonstrate beautifully two aspects of "the real"
that are worth talking about. The first of these aspects
is something that we have just been examining: the
impossibility of treating a convincing fiction as something other than flesh and blood. I am not trying here

to play at paradox. But the fact is it is true that a fiction frequently seems to us far more real than flesh and blood; for the fiction is, in one sense, truer to itself—simpler—than people ever can be. Almost all of our human problems—problems of living in the day-to-day world—seem to come out of that kind of a demand for simplification. What we cannot admit—sometimes even to ourselves—is the fact that we are not so much a core personality (a single "self" that has quite precise and definable characteristics) as a bundle of personalities, most of them similar to one another but none identical and all capable of extraordinary reversals. When we get mad at one another, each complains of the mask the other is wearing. But, in fact, what each is seeing in the other is obviously not mask but rather an aspect of self that he refuses to acknowledge as valid. We *are* what every situation demands. So that the man being kissed goodnight—at different times and at different places—by mother, wife, mistress, and child is, for all practical purposes, four personalities of the one body, none of them truer than the other.

What Durrell creates in the figure of Iolanthe—or rather in the figures of Iolanthe—is, first, a fictitious "live" woman who dies and, second, a fiction of that fictitious woman who, in search of freedom, is driven to suicide. And what disturbs us is that, like the characters in the book, we find ourselves drawn more easily to the second figure—the plastic and wire fiction—than to her presumably more real counterpart. She is easier to deal with because simpler, because purer than that other fiction, the "real" Iolanthe, had been. But, in fact, neither the flesh and blood Iolanthe nor the plastic Iolanthe is flesh and blood. Both are fictions, though the supremely fictitious, to adapt Wallace Stevens's phrase, is the more easily loved. After all, who doesn't feel a kind of love entangled with pathos whenever he talks to a beautiful woman made of nuts and bolts and gears and glop who is herself not only unaware of her composition but who would, if told of it, be totally incapable of accepting the possibility?

The second aspect of "the real" that Iolanthe helps make us aware of is its extraordinarily transient nature. For if "the real" exists primarily as a field observed and altered, it also exists only instantaneously. No one can live next year, or tomorrow, or, until it has become the present and instantly disappeared, one second from now. I clap my hands. You, I, all of us who heard that hand clap were alive during that instant but no longer will have the possibility ever again of being alive during that fraction of a second of sound that has already faded into silence. It's gone, and the aliveness that we had at that moment is gone with it. We can never get back there to live that time again or to revise any action that we took during that instant of lost time. All of that time—as I will soon be insisting in a short discussion of Beckett's *How It Is*—all of that time is irrevocable *was*.

Iolanthe, however, both in her flesh-and-blood self and in the plastic fiction of that dead body, is always caught up in an endlessly disappearing present. Because they are conscious of her as a machine that has taken on life, all of the characters of the book who speak to her are intensely aware—far more than any of us in life are normally aware—that she lives always on a razor edge of choice. Though she must not escape the "hospital" in which she has been brought back to life or the apartment where she is convalescent, though she must certainly be kept from a world that knows she died and was buried, finally no one is able to prevent her from taking the free action that sends her out into the

world and away from the people she feels have en-
trapped her. For in the long run, they cannot control
her. She makes, moment by moment, the decisions—
takes the free actions—that are available only during
the instant in which anyone is ever alive.

Though the pair of novels make the point conspicuously clear, Durrell—in a "Postface" note at the end
of *Nunquam*—stresses it. He remarks that his novels
had been once called "inquests with open verdicts" and
then goes on to allude to the passage from the *Satyricon*
of Petronius that acts as an epigraph for the second
book and that touches on both of them: "Aut tunc, aut
nunquam," "It was then or never. . . ." But by book's
end, *then* and *never* are utterly transformed; for the
past, as Durrell insists, has most meaning if seen not
as the *cause* of the present but, ironically, as the *result*
of it: our present choice—the instant choice accomplished in the clap of two palms against one another—
becomes the only past we will ever have. By the end,
then or never is abandoned in favor of more accurate
terminology. "It's always *now* or never," Durrell
says, "—since we are human and enjoy the fatality of
choice. Indeed the moment of choice is always now."

Beckett shares with Durrell and Green the sort of
cinematic observation, the focus on crucial instants,
and the awareness of the way in which the observer
alters the thing he observes and is in turn altered by it.
The tone of the work that he constructs is, however,
vastly different from Durrell's mixture of melodrama
and analysis and Henry Green's quiet, taut eloquence.

Because it so relentlessly focuses on a single figure
caught in a single action, I want to take as my example
Beckett's *How It Is*. Form in this book is the closest
any of these authors gets to the appearance of poetry.
The entire book is unpunctuated: no commas, no

periods, no semicolons, no dashes. Instead, it is broken
up into tiny paragraphs, some of them as short as a few
words, separated by large open spaces that represent,
perhaps, silence or—as the book jacket suggests—the
panting of the protagonist.

The title of the novel precisely describes its subject:
How It Is. It is a three-part novel about what turns out
to be a four-part subject: Before Pim, With Pim, After
Pim, and (unwritten) Before Someone-Who-Might-
as-Well-Be-Pim. It is an effort to see an apprehending
being caught in what Durrell would describe as the
flux of pure process.[8] The only thing he *knows* is what
he is: a naked old man crawling through mud. The
crawl is *How It Is,* and it continues—with interruptions
for sleep and the meeting with Pim—through the novel
and well past it into an entirely foreseeable future. The
crawl is presented to us literally hundreds of times in
words that have precious little (but that little precious)
variation. In the first section—*Before Pim*—it is inter-
rupted by images. These, Beckett points out, are not
memories, though at first he calls them that, because
the narrator is not at all sure that they belong to him.
That is, as he explains, he may be speaking in his own
voice, he may be quoting a voice that drones continually
in his ear, or both he and the voice may be a fiction
running through the head of someone else. In any event,
these images seem to the reader to be like scenes from
biography; they are, however, merely presented, not
interpreted. They are a part of how it is because they
happen in it. Here is an example from part one—the
very beginning, and a few of the images. Notice how
the present is constantly sustained as images intrude:

how it was I quote before Pim with Pim after Pim
how it is three parts I say it as I hear it

voice once without quaqua on all sides then in me
when the panting stops tell me again finish telling
me invocation

past moments old dreams back again or fresh like
those that pass or things things always and memories
I say them as I hear them murmur them in the mud

.   .   .   .

life in the light first image some creature or other I
watched him after my fashion from afar through my
spy-glass sidelong in mirrors through windows at
night first image

saying to myself he's better than he was better than
yesterday less ugly less stupid less cruel less dirty
less old less wretched and you saying to myself and
you bad to worse bad to worse steadily

something wrong there

or no worse saying to myself no worse you're no
worse and was worse

I pissed and shat another image in my crib never
so clean since

I scissored into slender strips the wings of butterflies
first one wing then the other sometimes for a change
the two abreast never so good since

that's all for the moment there I leave I hear it
murmur it to the mud there I leave for the moment
life in the light it goes out[9]

Part one ends with the narrator's discovery of Pim.
The narrator is, of course, still crawling through mud; but
a sack of food that he has been carrying has burst, and
his present crawl is in a zigzag chevron pattern, a design

calculated to increase his chances of running across something to eat:

> sudden swerve therefore left it's preferable forty-five degrees and two yards straight line such is the force of habit then right right angle and straight ahead four yards dear figures then left right angle and beeline four yards then right right angle so on till Pim[10]

Zigzagging along, the narrator alternately curses and blesses God, as he imagines an endless row of crawlers similar to himself—all of whom, he speculates, must have met his own burst-bag fate and so perhaps also accidentally have provided an "endless cortège of sacks burst in the interests of all." Filled with a mixture of hope, despair, prayer, and blasphemy, he zigzags on:

> semi-side right left leg left arm push pull flat on the face mute imprecations scrabble in the mud every half-yard eight times per chevron or three yards of headway clear a little less the hand dips clawing for the take instead of the familiar slime an arse two cries one mute end of part one before Pim that's how it was before Pim[11]

With Pim, the second part, concerns itself with the varieties of torture inflicted by the narrator on Pim— a naked little old man, whom the narrator instantly wraps in his arms, names with what may be his own name, and robs of his food. The torture is intended to force Pim to communicate—to tell his past. There is a reasonable chance, of course, that Pim's stories are all fictions; but they give the narrator some sense of otherness, of a self beyond himself. The torture that had been intended to keep Pim talking, however, eventually wears him out. At the very end of the second part Pim

disappears and the narrator is left alone stretched flat
on the mud.

As part three starts, the narrator discovers another
sack of food and remembers that before part one he
had been tortured by someone named Bem, who gave
him a name, took his food, and forced him to recall or
invent a past. At this point, he realizes that someone
else, perhaps someone he will call Bom, will arrive,
this time to torture him as Bem had and as he had
tortured Pim. So the pattern becomes clear to him: crawl
alone, torture, sprawl alone, be tortured, crawl alone,
torture, on and on, forever. This eventually is worked
out as a universal pattern:

> at the instant I leave Bem another leaves Pim and
> let us be at that instant one hundred thousand strong
> then fifty thousand departures fifty thousand aban-
> doned no sun no earth nothing turning the same
> instant always everywhere

> at the instant I reach Pim another reaches Bem we
> are regulated thus our justice wills it thus fifty thou-
> sand couples again at the same instant the same
> everywhere with the same space between them it's
> mathematical it's our justice in this muck where all
> is identical our ways and way of faring right leg
> right arm push pull

> as long as I with Pim the other with Bem a hundred
> thousand prone glued two by two together vast
> stretch of time nothing stirring save the tormentors
> those whose turn it is on and off right arm claw
> the armpit for the song carve the scriptions plunge
> the opener pestle the kidney all the needful

> at the instant Pim leaves me and goes towards the
> other Bem leaves the other and comes towards me

I place myself at my point of view migration of
slime-worms then or tailed latrinal scissiparous
frenzy days of great gaiety

at the instant Pim reaches the other to form again
with him the only couple he forms apart from the one
with me Bem reaches me to form with me the only
couple he forms apart from the one with the other[12]

The end of the book, "How It Is," is set in the mud,
the narrator waiting for his torturer to arrive and
speculating as to whether this world he lives in is God
ordained, an elaborate structure carefully designed with
food strategically placed in the mud and the roles of
alternate tormenter and tormented deliberately schema-
tized, or whether instead other realities can be con-
ceived—whether, for example, there might be other
worlds

as just as ours but less exquisitely organized

one perhaps there is one perhaps somewhere merciful
enough to shelter such frolics where no one ever
abandons anyone and no one ever waits for anyone
and never two bodies touch[13]

And finally he explores the possibility that the world is
utterly solipsistic, a world in which one is both torturer
and victim, speaker and spoken to. The narrator handles
it, as elsewhere, in a kind of catechism:

in the familiar form of questions I am said to ask
myself and answers I am said to give myself however
unlikely that may appear last scraps very last when
the panting stops last murmurs very last however
unlikely that may appear

.   .   .   .

only me yes alone yes with my voice yes my murmur
yes when the panting stops yes all that holds yes
panting yes worse and worse no answer WORSE
AND WORSE yes flat on my belly yes in the mud yes
the dark yes nothing to emend there no the arms
spread yes like a cross no answer LIKE A CROSS no
answer YES OR NO yes

never crawled no in an amble no right leg right arm
push pull ten yards fifteen yards no never stirred
no never made to suffer no never suffered no answer
NEVER SUFFERED no never abandoned no never was
abandoned no so that's life here no answer THAT'S
MY LIFE HERE screams good

alone in the mud yes the dark yes sure yes panting
yes someone hears me no no one hears me no mur-
muring sometimes yes when the panting stops yes not
at other times no in the mud yes to the mud yes my
voice yes mine yes not another's no mine alone
yes sure yes when the panting stops yes on and off
yes a few words yes a few scraps yes that no one
hears no but less and less no answer LESS AND LESS
yes

so things may change no answer end no answer I
may choke no answer sink no answer sully the mud
no more no answer the dark no answer trouble the
peace no more no answer the silence no answer
die no answer DIE screams I MAY DIE screams I
SHALL DIE screams good

good good end at last of part three and last that's
how it was end of quotation after Pim how it is[14]

If we are left here with a reality that is self-projected,
we must also remember that the reality of part one

was full of "images"—scenes of moments of conventional living—and that the entirety of part two saw reality as pure interrelationship, Pim and the narrator existing only in terms of each other and neither meaningful without the other. The design of the three parts, in this sense, is to present three of the possible varieties of being, of the kinds of *is-ness* available to us.

Finally, I want to return to Henry Green. What I intend to do is to quote rather an extended passage from *Loving* and to ask you to recall the James Wright poem with which I started this discussion: Wright's moment of stopped time in which two friends watch two horses nuzzle each other in a meadow, a poem that ends with an abruptly felt and enormously powerful emotion:

> Suddenly I realize
> That if I stepped out of my body I would break
> Into blossom.

Time, in Wright's poem, is stopped—cameralike—just long enough for that important, oblique feeling to define itself. The poem is a shutter snapping on a scene precisely as a feeling discovers itself.

And I also have to ask you to recall my examples from Keats and Joyce of cinematic treatment of a scene—the complex nature of reality revealed by the shifting focus of lenses that offer us panorama, detail, close detail, closest detail, and panorama again. Finally, I have to ask you to recall Wallace Stevens's three agents—daytime wood-dove, nighttime astrologer, and day-and-night ocean—all howling their various *hoos* and allowing us to discover the "strange relation" with which life's nonsense pierces us.

Loving, like *How It Is,* is accurately described by its title and reminds one a little of Durrell's *Alexandria*

Quartet, not so much in its form but in its concern
with all the varieties of love open to man's endlessly
inventive, exploratory nature. For it touches on most
of love's manifestations: friendship, courtship, com-
radeship, marriage; paternal and maternal love; puppy
love, senile adoration, homosexuality, random animal
promiscuity, incest, adultery—even frigidity, if that's a
form of love, as I suppose in the negative universe it
really must be.

More to our purpose, however, *Loving* sets up against
a series of very brief scenes moments that strike us as
stopped in time. While that stoppage occurs, Green
draws on overlapping imagery like that used by
Stevens—in the passage that I shall soon be quoting,
for example, imagery associated with the color gold—
to create a resonant universe full of unexpected, echoing
significance. Irrational relationships abruptly exist. Life's
nonsense, to combine phrases from two of the authors
we have been examining, in the end draws tears out
of the stone. Sometimes these relationships are obvious,
easily defined—like long light cast on things at evening,
shadows that a group of standing stones no taller than
a man cast across an entire Irish valley on, say, a late
September afternoon you or I or Henry Green might
once have known.

But consider another kind of more complex overlap:
in the upcoming passage, an entanglement of mouse
references and the phrase "treasure from the bog." The
first time the phrase appears is some twenty pages
earlier in the novel.[15] There, it is associated with Captain Davenport. Davenport, an amateur archeologist,
has been in the habit of making love to the daughter-
in-law of the owner of a disintegrating but still-inhab-
ited Irish castle in which the entire action of the novel

takes place. The scene of their affair—the bog in which he searches for treasures—has been accidentally pinpointed by a stuck weather indicator. The indicator is stuck because a mouse is caught in its clockwork machinery. When the seduced lady discovers the wind-direction arrow rigidly pointing to the bog site, she becomes so upset that she rips the pointer from the wall.

Most of the book, however, is concerned not with the affairs of the owners of the castle but rather with those of their servants, among them Paddy O'Conor, an Irishman who supervises a flock of peacocks but who in the eyes of most of the characters of the novel is dirty, middle-aged, and misshapen; Charley Raunce, who discovers the mouse in the clockworks, a forty-year-old butler strongly attached to his mother but by the end of the book engaged; and Kate and Edith, two young maids who lead Charley to the panel behind which mouse and clockwork have conspired to turn the ever-shifting wind into an unshifting accusation and who themselves have a strong but unacknowledged lesbian attachment that they pass off to each other as playful girlish affection in a household of much older men and women. Kate, the more sophisticated of the two girls, decides that she can come to love Paddy when she learns that Edith has fallen in love with Charley and intends, at novel's end, to marry him.

All these relationships are very delicately suggested rather than explicitly spelled out. Green doesn't describe such feelings—or even name them, in most instances; rather, he lets the imagery insinuate them into a territory somewhere at the back of our minds. The scene that follows allows us to see Kate showing her own image of Paddy to Edith. In one sense, the entire book is a spy story, and, as this scene opens, Mrs. Welch, the

cook, is spying on the two girls through a hole in the
wall of the kitchen larder. Mice, golden light, treasure
from a bog, and other echoing material help give the
passage its special quality of stopped but stretched
time:

> The back premises of this grey castle were on a
> vast scale. What she saw afar was Kate and Edith
> with their backs to her in purple uniforms and caps
> the colour of a priest's cassock. They seemed to be
> waiting outside O'Conor's lamp room. This was two
> tall Gothic windows and a pointed iron-studded door
> in a long wall of other similar doors and windows
> topped by battlements above which was set back
> another wall with a greater number of windows which
> in its turn was terraced into the last story that was
> almost all blind Gothic windows under a steep roof
> of slate. Mrs. Welch, after seeming to linger over the
> great shaft of golden sun which lighted these girls
> through parted cloud, let a great gust of sigh and
> turned away saying, "Well if Aggie Burch can't
> hold 'em in leash it's none of my business, the pair
> of two-legged mice, the thieves," she added.
>
> But as Edith reached for O'Conor's latch Kate
> screamed at her, "And what if there's a mouse?"
> Then Edie, hands to the side over a swelling heart,
> gave back, "Oh love, you can't say that to me," and
> leaned against the doorpost. "That you can't say,
> love," she said, dizzy once more all of a sudden.
> "Aw come on I only meant it for a game." [16]

The girls are for a moment startled by a peacock
that seems to be staring at them, but they are relieved
to find he has his "one black white-rimmed eye" fixed
on a buzzard. Edgy, they debate whether to spy on

O'Conor, who after all, they fear, may not really be
"asleep in the dark." Finally Kate gathers up her nerve
and raises the heavy latch of the door:

> "But love I'll never cause a sound even the smallest,"
> she said low. Edith plastered her mouth over with
> the palm of a hand.
> "No," she said muffled, "no," as O'Conor's life
> was opened, as Kate let the sun in and Edith bent
> to look.
> What they saw was a saddleroom which dated
> back to the time when there had been guests out
> hunting from Kinalty. It was a place from which
> light was almost excluded now by cobwebs across its
> two windows and into which, with the door ajar,
> the shafted sun lay in a lengthened arch of blazing
> sovereigns. Over a corn bin on which he had packed
> last autumn's ferns lay Paddy snoring between these
> windows, a web strung from one lock of hair back
> onto the sill above and which rose and fell as he
> breathed. Caught in the reflection of spring sunlight
> this cobweb looked to be made of gold as did those
> others which by working long minutes spiders had
> drawn from spar to spar of the fern bedding on
> which his head rested. It might have been almost that
> O'Conor's dreams were held by hairs of gold binding
> his head beneath a vaulted roof on which the floor
> of cobbles reflected an old king's molten treasure
> from the bog.[17]

Edith voices what the reader has already apprehended,
that O'Conor—who is, as she says, "a sight and all"
—has begun to take on majesty. Under the golden light,
a ragged Irishman has for one magical moment come
into his lost inheritance. Though they joke and laugh,
they know that a ritual gesture is demanded of them

and they start to go through the ceremonies that could perhaps restore a sleeping prince to his proper kingdom.

"If I make a crown out of them ferns in the corner," Edith said, "will you fetch something he can hold?"

"You aim to make him a bishop? Well if I'ad my way I'd strip those rags off to give that pelt of his a good rub over."

"Don't talk so. You couldn't."

"Who's doing all the talking?" O'Conor gave a loud snore. Both girls began to giggle.

"Oh do be quiet dear," Edith said, picking a hand- ful of ferns and starting to twist them. Then they were arrested by movement in the sunset of that sidewall which reflected glare from the floor in its glass.

For most of one side of this room was taken up by a vast glass-fronted cupboard in which had once been kept the bits, the halters and bridles, and the martin- gales. At some time O'Conor had cut away wooden partitioning at the back to make a window into the next chamber, given over nowadays to his peacocks. This was where these birds sheltered in winter, nested in spring, and where they died of natural causes at the end. As though stuffed in a dusty case they showed themselves from time to time as one after another across the heavy days they came up to look at him. Now, through a veil of light reflected over this plate glass from beneath, Edith could dimly see, not hear, a number of peacocks driven into view by some disturbance on their side and hardly to be recognized in this sovereign light. For their eyes had changed to rubies, their plumage to orange as they bowed and scraped at each other against the equal danger. Then again they were gone with a beat of wings, and in their room stood Charley Raunce, the skin of his pale face altered by refraction to red morocco leather.

The girls stood transfixed as if by arrows between the Irishman dead motionless asleep and the other intent and quiet behind a division. Then, dropping everything, they turned, they also fled.[18]

The book opens with the phrase "Once upon a day" and it ends with the phrase "lived happily ever after," so we know we are seeing something more than naturalism though, oddly, reviewers praised the book for its "accurate" picture of servant life. What we have here —thanks to the intrusion of gold light into a spiderweb kingdom—is an echo of *Sleeping Beauty.* And, in apprehending that echo, we discover once more that reality is only what eyes see and that their shifting lenses give us an endlessly varied version of the magic richness of what is—a shifting, endlessly surprising, interpenetrating world of possibility in which, observing well, we are constantly pierced by the flickering discoveries of life's nonsense correlations. We see a field littered with standing stones that remind us of persons. "Nonsense," we say, acknowledging the whole poem of the real that is spread out there before us like a fragment of torn film.

Notes

1. James Wright, *The Branch Will Not Break* (Middleton, Conn.: Wesleyan University Press, 1963), p. 57. Copyright © 1961 by James Wright. Reprinted from *The Branch Will Not Break,* by James Wright, by permission of

Wesleyan University Press. "A Blessing" first appeared in *Poetry*.

2. Henry Green, *Pack My Bag* (London: Hogarth Press, 1940), pp. 7–8.

3. Ibid., p. 211.

4. Lawrence Durrell, *A Key to Modern British Poetry* (Norman: University of Oklahoma Press, 1952), pp. 29–30.

5. Wallace Stevens, *The Collected Poems of Wallace Stevens* (New York: Alfred A. Knopf, 1955), p. 383.

6. Green, *Pack My Bag,* p. 88.

7. Lawrence Durrell, *Nunquam* (New York: Dutton, 1970), p. 319.

8. See, for example, the end of Durrell's play, *An Irish Faustus* (New York: Dutton, 1964), pp. 86 ff.

9. Samuel Beckett, *How It Is* (New York: Grove Press, 1964), pp. 7, 9.

10. Ibid., p. 47.

11. Ibid., p. 48.

12. Ibid., pp. 112–113.

13. Ibid., p. 143.

14. Ibid., pp. 144, 146–147.

15. Henry Green, *Loving* (New York: Viking Press, 1949), p. 32.

16. Ibid., pp. 52–53.

17. Ibid., pp. 53–54.

18. Ibid., pp. 54–55.

Appendix

A Panel Discussion

MODERATOR: Alan Warren Friedman

PARTICIPANTS:

James Cowan   Avrom Fleishman
James Gindin   J. Hillis Miller
Charles Rossman   John Unterecker

MEMBERS OF THE AUDIENCE:

Bryan Dobbs   Joseph Doherty
Joseph Kruppa   Gordon Mills
John Velz   Carl Wood

Introduction

Alan Warren Friedman

Despite what may at times appear something of a hodgepodge approach, I would like to suggest a principle behind what many of us have tried to accomplish in recent years and this week. Perhaps the way to begin is by asking what sort of perversity it is that defines the modern period as stretching back one hundred years and extends British literature to encompass virtually any artistic product written in the English language

anywhere—except perhaps in the United States? A
rather useful perversity, I should think, for it permits
the creation of a good English department, not through
meticulous program planning but through the hiring
of good faculty members. It builds an extraordinary,
if not unique, special collections library, not through
filling gaps but by wholesale acquiring of available
private collections. And it fosters a high-quality symposium by bringing together good speakers and good
moderators and good audiences and setting them free
to dream in public, as it were, to define their own way
within a broad topic broadly defined. If the modern
British novel is written in the latter part of the nineteenth century, or in Trieste and New Mexico and
Egypt, or by Anglo-Irishmen born in India, or by ex-
patriate Irishmen writing in France and French—well,
so be it, so it goes, and so much the better for modern
British fiction.

We have learned this week not only about tradition
and the individual talent, but also something of breadth,
of an extraordinary spectrum of possibilities: the kind
of questions we have asked concern ethics and aesthetics,
metaphysics and epistemology, the uses and possibilities of history, the logic of causality, the nature of
mimesis, and the données of genres. Whether defined
in terms that are called ethical, Apollonian, religious,
literary, legendary, or mythical, continuity has its impact—especially when it runs smack up against that
special kind of tradition that might be called presentism
or, in Hardy's phrase, the "ache of modernism," and
that has been enshrined in a living monument, that
newest and most elusive of literary genres whose
parameters we have found it convenient to assume this
week. Yet as Percy Lubbock warned us back in 1921
in *The Craft of Fiction* (New York: Viking Press, pp.

1–3), the novel continually eludes us: "To grasp the
shadowy and fantasmal form of a book, to hold it fast,
to turn it over and survey it at leisure—that is the
effort of a critic of books, and it is perpetually defeated.
Nothing, no power, will keep a book steady and motionless before us, so that we may have time to examine
its shape and design. As quickly as we read, it melts
and shifts in the memory; even at the moment when
the last page is turned, a great part of the book, its finer
detail, is already vague and doubtful. . . . The form of a
novel—and how often a critic uses that expression,
too—is something that none of us, perhaps, has ever
really contemplated. It is revealed little by little, page
by page, and it is withdrawn as fast as it is revealed; as
a whole, complete and perfect, it could only exist in a
more tenacious memory than most of us have to rely
on. Our critical faculty may be admirable; we may be
thoroughly capable of judging a book justly, if only
we could watch it at ease. But fine taste and keen perception are of no use to us if we cannot retain the image
of the book; and the image escapes and evades us like
a cloud."

Our frustration is perhaps compounded by efforts
made to convince us of the moribundity of the novel—
efforts that predate, and will no doubt postdate, the
McLuhan phenomenon. Yet I find pronouncements of
the novel's demise, like Twain's and God's, rather premature. Like the temporally identical rising middle
class, the novel is forever in motion; it will be dead in
the unlikely time when the rising middle class is in
fact risen. For the time being, the novel's death, like
God's in Yeats's phrase, is "but a play"—a ritual, a
public performance, something we need to go through
in order to initiate the cycle that allows us to need and
experience it yet again, to make it again new. Such

projections upon reality are stocks-in-trade of those
for whom abstractions like death and marriage are
simply terminal and who, along with Hamlet, can speak
of "that undiscovered country from whose bourne no
traveller ever returns" while the ghost who *has* returned struts and frets upon the stage before him and
us. Such dying and death are immediate and real, incessant, like the season, the day, the hour, a way of meas-
uring, an instrument of definition. Lawrence Durrell
writes that "time is the measure of our death-con-
sciousness. There are other organisms, we know, which
measure time by a heat-unit. They must have a different
idea of death. Then there are those so-called simple
cells which multiply by binary fission—they simply
divide into two. You might say one dies into two,
leaving no corpse behind it as a human being does.
Does the caterpillar die to become a moth or would
you call it being born? We do not know. In some cases
birth and death would seem to be almost interchange-
able terms" (*A Key to Modern British Poetry,* Norman:
University of Oklahoma Press, 1952, p. 4).

What this week's papers have demonstrated is that
the novel's dying is no cause for despair or concern;
for how else shall novelists, like craftsmen and critics,
be forever making it new—always broader in scope
and subject matter, finer and more expansive, always
immediate and beyond, risking skimming the vital
surfaces with Galsworthy, immersing into destructive
elements with Conrad, taking Daedalian flight with
Joyce, daring to demand of us, at one end, the radical
compassion of Hardy's *Tess of the d'Urbervilles* or, at
the other, the formalistic disorientations of Beckett's
fictions? Like many of its modern practitioners, the
novel itself has what has been called "an encyclopedic
style." Yet what else should we expect, what less should

we demand, from a mode of communication in whose name eclectic innovativeness and incessant revitalizing are absorbed and proclaimed?

Finally and as a means of initiating discussion, I would like to ask what we are to say of the vitality of a genre whose poetics is virtually contemporary? Even the idea of such a poetics antedates our century hardly at all; in 1884 Henry James refers to such a notion in much the same defensive tone we might expect from an attempt to define a poetics of television soap operas today. James speaks of his "temerity" in affixing such a comprehensive title as "The Art of Fiction" (in *The Future of the Novel,* ed. Leon Edel, New York: Vintage Books, pp. 3–5) "to these few remarks . . . Only a short time ago it might have been supposed that the English novel was not what the French call *discutable.* It had no air of having a theory, a conviction, a consciousness of itself behind it—of being the expression of an artistic faith, the result of choice and comparison. . . . there was a comfortable, good-humored feeling abroad that a novel is a novel, as a pudding is a pudding, and that our only business with it could be to swallow it." And though James is optimistic about the current and future state of novel criticism and theory, what he calls "discussion, suggestion, formulation," he nonetheless feels compelled to proceed by defending the novel against some rather old canards: that it is "wicked," that it is only a "make-believe," that it is untruthful. Despite the important laying out done by James himself, and then by Ford and Conrad, Lubbock and E. M. Forster, Lawrence and Woolf, it seems to me that only in the last two decades has theorizing about the novel reached something of a culmination though not a termination; for the work of Wayne Booth and Robert Scholes, of Richard Ellmann and Hugh Kenner, of Mark

Schorer and Leon Edel, of Ian Watt and Leslie Fiedler, along with that of many others, including our panelists, suggests to me a questioning, an opening outward, a trembling on the verge (to use Virginia Woolf's phrase in a rather different way), that is every bit as daring and resonant as that proclaimed by the modern novel itself. If this is true, does it then mean that the novel is indeed alive and well, or is a poetics performed only after the fact, like an autopsy? What I am asking, then, is not only where is British fiction now that it has defined a modern tradition, say from Hardy to Durrell, but also where is it now that it has inspired something of a poetics, say from Henry James to John Unterecker?

FLEISHMAN: John, did I take you to say that change is of the essence in fiction?

UNTERECKER: Not of the essence; that it happens. In other words, I think that notions of form just *do* evolve. Change is something that is inescapable and to assume that a form will stay forever fixed is, I think, one of the critical dangers that we are always falling into. I think, for instance, of the messes that people got into in Elizabethan times, people who got terribly up-tight about theories of tragedy, for example. And if a tragedy did not conform to the theoretical version or what they understood to be the theoretical version of Greek tragedy passed through Latin tragedy, then it was bad because it didn't fit the critical model. And I think the critical model is always in danger of being an oversimplification of the sprawling fact. What we have to keep our eye on is that amorphous crawling thing that is indeed the fiction.

FLEISHMAN: And yet, in the account you gave of a number of novels, very beautifully done I must say, the world seemed static. There was time at a moment,

to which you accorded a high degree of reality, its in-
stantaneity; then later there was a moment of consider-
ing that past moment, also a static moment itself (time
seemed to have dropped out), and I wonder whether
change drops out of the novel, as you were describing
it.

UNTERECKER: What I think happens is that
those kinds of pauses that I was trying to suggest do
happen in certain novelists (conspicuously in Green
and sometimes in Beckett and sometimes in Durrell)
—those times when you simply stop time to look at it,
when you freeze a moment, and from the frozen moment certain kinds of feelings can define themselves. I
think that those become little peaks that appear in the
thing. I don't mean to suggest that those things, those
pauses, those breaks, are the real novel. The real novel
involves a flow, but just as the scene can be narrowed
down or spread out, so time can be stopped or speeded
up.

FLEISHMAN: Are those the poet's moments
within the novel?

UNTERECKER: I think that those often become
the moments that resemble the way a poet operates.
And I think that a lot of novelists in the twentieth
century, at least, have taken a cue from a certain kind
of poetry. I was trying to give an image of two kinds
of poetry, one of them a kind of Keatsian flow that I
was trying to suggest in "The Eve of St. Agnes," a kind
of poetry that still seems to me cinematic. And another
kind of poetry seems to me static, like a fixed photograph, a still, as I was trying to suggest with the Wright
poem. And I think novels use both of those, in a sense,
photographic techniques. Rather alternately, at that.

FLEISHMAN: I think I understand that.

GINDIN: While you were talking about the novels

historically, and talking about novels representing change, it seemed, in the way you look at novels of the past, that the change, though to some extent continuous, has a huge wrench or S-curve somewhere in the twenties or so. I wondered about this, because then you seemed to take something quite different in the novel —"realism," "naturalism," and you used terms of that sort. And yet, as I think back about the nineteenth century, I become increasingly skeptical about what "realism" or "naturalism" could have meant, and I wonder if a word like *realism* is only a word we can use about the past. We can say that writers at some point in the past were realistic, yet, had we been Victorians, we would not have seen any Victorian novel as realistic. We would have had the same questions about the reality a given novel depicted that we have about the kind of reality that contemporary authors depict.

For example, Hillis Miller was saying that *Wuthering Heights* would become a very difficult kind of novel to apply a single, critical point of view to. And I think I would certainly agree. Obviously we couldn't call that realistic. We often say that someone like Trollope is realistic, but it seems to me that that's simply because he doesn't write with metaphors. Was that real Victorian life? We don't know that, in any real sense, either. And so I wonder if, given your sort of idea of change as having a wrench in it, we can only talk about that fiction before the wrench in static critical terms because these are terms—

UNTERECKER: Because we're after it.

GINDIN: —because we're after it, yes. These are ex post facto terms entirely.

UNTERECKER: The only thing I would answer is that I think that at certain times novelists do associate themselves with a critical school, as certainly

Zola associated himself with the idea of naturalism; that is, he had an idea of what he was trying to do, and he called it naturalism. So that, I suppose, we would have to say that those people who associated themselves with that word, in a sense trying to do that, who thought of themselves as naturalists and thought that the job of naturalism was to account for a present—which I think is pretty much what naturalism sets out to do— those novelists are, in a sense, asking to be judged in those terms. But I was really trying to suggest that those terms, not just in our own time, but even in terms of the past, seem to us pretty sleazy terms now. And I think that we don't find large talk in very simple ways about naturalism, say, versus symbolism anymore. If we have eyes we can see, for example, that *Madame Bovary* is simultaneously a symbolist and a realistic novel. And so, for that matter, is Joyce, who used to be lumped for a long time as pure symbolist. But what's more realistic, or naturalistic, than a lot of those passages in *Ulysses* and in *Dubliners?*

So, it just seems to me that what's happened is that convenient terms of the past have suddenly become inconvenient. That's all I'm really saying. I was really quite bowled over by what you were saying yesterday, Hillis (that is, bowled over by being attracted to it) — the notion of the novel as a thing of repetitions. It was something that I'd at one point considered making; in fact, one of my abandoned papers had rather a long stretch on the repetitions in the poem and the repetitions in the novel being terribly similar. And certain writers really made that the core of their kind of novel. And what made it most attractive to me was your assertion that we can't say that a particular way of reading those repetitions becomes *the* core. That is, I think that what goes wrong with a lot of symbolist criticism is

that we'll say, "Ah, here is *the* symbol," and all of a
sudden the novel is made to conform to a critic's version
of what the symbol is, which becomes larger than the
novel. And I don't think that, as critics, we dare do
that. I found your notion of taking any point in the
network as a possible point of departure marvelous.

MILLER: Since you've been generous to me, I
feel sort of curmudgeonly to challenge something in
your paper, for which I share Avrom's admiration; but
it is an occasion to say that I've been worried in the
papers by—I don't quite know how to phrase this—
by the way we've all tended to assume that there *is*
something special about the twentieth century, as your
paper in a way does. It's partly me trying to defend
my Victorians. But I think there's a little more to it
than that. I would like to suggest an alternative way of
thinking about periods to the one that I think we all
habitually have: and that is of setting the sort of
young, naïvely realistic Victorians against us liberated
twentieth-century people.

This kind of thinking I find more and more unper-
suasive—not because it isn't the case that the theory
of fiction of the Victorian period was pretty stupid, but
because of the actual practice of the novelists. I was
listening to your paper and thinking of the cinematic
thing and feeling that you're right about Keats. But
you could say the same thing about the opening of
Bleak House, which is marvelously cinematic (we
know, in fact, it influenced Eisenstein and the way he
thought of making films), or of the cinematic aspects
of Hardy, whose novels often read like a scenario, at
least for places in *The Mayor of Casterbridge,* which
has sort of a wide shot that moves then down into
the village of Casterbridge, and so on. And this was
before movies existed.

So, there is obviously a very curious relationship between the cinema and the novel that you can't explain by saying that the movies influenced modern fiction.

UNTERECKER: For that matter, Shakespeare wrote better movie scripts than he did plays.

MILLER: Something like that. It's really myself that I'm worried about here as much as the rest of us. Any generalizations that you make, such as the generalization about Victorian fiction I tried to make in *The Form of Victorian Fiction,* is completely demolished by certain texts like *Don Quixote* or like *Tristram Shandy* or like *Wuthering Heights* in the Victorian period, which don't fit any generalizations you could make about them at all. And almost anything one can say about narrative fiction that suggests there's been an increase in sophistication in any way is, it seems to me, completely put in question by the oldest novel of all, by Cervantes.

I am wondering if an alternative way to think about this wouldn't be to say, without denying the differences between modern fiction and nineteenth-century fiction and eighteenth-century fiction, that there has been from the beginning of what we think of as modern fiction, which I guess goes back to the Renaissance, a certain set of techniques of narrative: for example, the illusion of perspectivism, the use of stories within stories, the time shift, all the things we think of as being technical devices—the use of poetic language, of figures of speech or symbol, the whole works. It's there, I think, from the beginning. And that what, in fact, constitutes the specificity of a given period is not something entirely new that involves a rejection of what was before but a kind of special arrangement of these techniques in a given period.

UNTERECKER: Or perhaps a conscious formulation of them somewhere along the line. That is, when you were saying that the criticism of the nineteenth century seemed unsophisticated, this is heartily agreed, though the works themselves are sophisticated works. And maybe the works are not so dramatically different, although I do think there is still a shade of reflection of thought in the works.

MILLER: They're different. On the other hand, you couldn't tell the George Eliot of *Middlemarch*— not in her theory about the novel, although there is an extraordinary little essay about form that sounds very twentieth century in its notions about form and its rejection of the idea of organic form—anything about perspectivism that Durrell would have to teach her. That's a novel about perspectivism, which seems to me quite passable—without denying that *Middlemarch* doesn't really sound like *The Alexandria Quartet;* that's why I think the idea of the rearrangement of the same techniques might be better than the old notion of a sort of self-enclosed period, which is then gone beyond by something that renders it obsolete.

UNTERECKER: I didn't really want to suggest that notion of rendering obsolete. I was trying to suggest that what happens is a shift, but that you don't eliminate the previous world. What changes is a way of looking and the way of looking may be in fact far more in critical eyes than in novelistic practice. But the way of looking does change.

FLEISHMAN: Could we say that what changes, the new element in present novelists' perspective, is their consciousness of the novelists of the past: simply the fact that those novels have been written, have instructed the practitioner of modern style, and yet have seemed inadequate to him, to the novel he wants to write, makes them then part of the new novel that he writes. Not necessarily departing from it, even when he wants to, even when he declares it his program to do so. I think with Woolf, with Joyce, that there are very conscious efforts to be truer to psychology, to be truer to the flow of human experience in fiction than has previously been done, but, in the very effort to make fictional work of such treatments of human experience, they come back to realistic and other conventions and create a new mix.

MILLER: That's a very good notion. One could add to that the fact that it's by way of Proust and Joyce and so on that we read George Eliot now and see things that are really *there,* but that are, in a way, developed like a photographic film by the later writers. I think this is for me one of the ways in which Proust is so important. Proust's great novel, in a sense, is a kind of summary of the techniques of nineteenth-century fiction, including English fiction with the tremendous influence on Proust of George Eliot and Hardy. One of the critical remarks about those, in a way, leaves one, after Proust has written his novel, to read those novels differently and see things in them that people certainly didn't see in the nineteenth-century criticism.

UNTERECKER: And, in one sense, *How It Is* becomes an almost explicit commentary on Proust.

MILLER: That's right.

UNTERECKER: It's an extraordinary book in that respect because it watches Beckett come, in a funny way, full circle. He had started out by writing an essay on Proust, and then, as an old man, he turned again to precisely a Proustian problem, which is the problem of recall.

MILLER: That's right.

COWAN: I think one thing that is emerging from

this discussion is that we must not reify the idea you were speaking of, the Renaissance theorists on tragedy creating a static idea of what tragedy is; and obviously a viable art can't operate within such a static ideational framework. I think what's emerging here is that we mustn't do this to the novel. You know, the passage from Henry James that Alan quoted about how people have formerly thought of the novel as something like a pudding: you thought nothing except to swallow it. In *Alice's Adventures in Wonderland*—or perhaps *Through the Looking Glass*—Alice is introduced to a pudding and finds that she can't swallow someone to whom she hasn't been introduced properly. I think that *we* mustn't introduce our students to certain reified notions of what the novel is or of what critical concepts are, including our own critical concepts.

UNTERECKER: I'm sorry to have burst out laughing, but I am still remembering Iolanthe—and one of the problems for the character, Felix, in that book (who has after all put her together out of various bits of wire and plastic) is that Iolanthe suggests to him that they go to bed together and he realizes, of course, that they can but *he* can't because he, after all, has constructed her. And so the answer is that perhaps you can't go to bed with the woman you've made.

[Laughter]

GINDIN: Maybe, then, from what we've been saying, this change is more a change in our critical formulations, our critical consciousness about the novel in that as—

COWAN: Or about the novelists' consciousness about themselves.

GINDIN: Yes. And this, of course, becomes self-critical as well. And so we now find ourselves operating in a culture in which novelists are self-conscious critics

of self-conscious novelists and therefore have to deal
with a kind of awareness that's both historical and
critical. I don't think this means that their novels are
any the less complicated or any the less interesting, but
just that, in talking about them, we have to grapple
with a great many more terms, both puddings and
rules—these are both always involved.

FRIEDMAN: Perhaps this is the appropriate time
to throw it open to questions from the floor, now that
things have been laid bare up here to an extent.

Are there questions? Or comments? Or suggestions?
Yes?

MEMBER OF THE AUDIENCE: Don't you
think that the great difference between prose and poetry
still exists, and—although in many works of modern
prose you find very beautiful pieces of poetry, such as
you find in Joyce's *The Dead* and also in Virginia
Woolf or in many other writers—still there is a very
great difference between prose and poetry, that poetry
often after it is made stands like a plastic thing, right
in front of us, something vertical; it stays there and it
doesn't disappear? But in the case of, let's say *How It Is,*
you move from Pim to not-Pim. In other words, this
goes on: there is a kind of subconscious chronology
that takes you along; there is a kind of sequence of
events that you don't find in poetry. You may find it,
of course, in narrative poetry, but you don't find it in
poetry per se, the genre itself.

UNTERECKER: I think what I was really interested in was the similarity of ways of holding a work
together that certain poets, at least, have used and that
certain novelists used. I think, too, that novelists in the
twentieth century—Virginia Woolf I would cite, for
example—have used devices that are easier to get at
in poetry, and perhaps that's what I meant by fiction at

the edge of poetry. I didn't mean that it *was* poetry—
or even was becoming poetry—but that it was at the
edge of it and that the machinery by which a poem is
held together and the machinery by which some of the
novels are held together are remarkably close.

Now, the experience of the novel and the experience,
say, of a lyric are I think vastly different. But the experience of moments in the novel become rather like
the experience of certain kinds of lyric. That was really
all I was trying to suggest—and that the novelists, I
think, at that point are really rather conscious of the
fact that they are using elements that we usually think
of as poetic. I'm not trying to suggest that you have a
merging of forms, but I don't really see that that's bad
either, when I get right down to it. Again, I think that
the mechanical divisions of form are critical achievements rather than literary achievements and that what
the writers do is always more protean and sloppier than
what the critics see them do.

MILLS: Mr. Unterecker, when you use the word
moments are you quoting from Virginia Woolf?

UNTERECKER: I wasn't quoting her. I think I
mean pretty much what she meant, but I wasn't quoting
her. I do think, though, it comes very close to what she
was talking about.

KRUPPA: I'm a little bit worried about the tendency on the part of some members of the panel
discussion to act as if a slight rearrangement of categories is what's going on in modern fiction.

MILLER: That's what I want to say; that's right.
You don't agree with that? Show me something in the
twentieth century that doesn't already exist in earlier
narrative forms, and then I'll agree with you.

KRUPPA: William Burroughs.

MILLER: Sure. It's there already in Rabelais.

UNTERECKER : All of it?

FLEISHMAN : I forget who it was who said we moderns are in such an unusual position because we know so much more than they did. And the rejoinder is, "Precisely, and they are that which we know."

WOOD : In dealing in generalities for a minute, I wonder if I can bring up the subject of a great age of literature, which seems to have arisen and declined in the last hundred years in modern British fiction as well as in modern American fiction and elsewhere. I wonder if you would agree that the quality of fiction that was produced by Woolf and Joyce is not being produced at the moment and has not been produced in the last couple of decades. We have at least a hint through Virginia Woolf's essay on "Mr. Bennett and Mrs. Brown" how this great period of literature might have come to rise, but no one has written an essay on why it might have concluded. I wonder if any of you would be willing to speculate on some of the reasons that might have brought modern or contemporary literature to its present stage of what I presume is a considerably lower quality than books in the time of Joyce.

COWAN : I will state one reason and one only and that is that a great many of the novelists of the last twenty to thirty years, despite such examples as those that Mr. Unterecker was dealing with this afternoon, have reacted against the experimentation of Woolf, Joyce, Lawrence, and *their* generation and have written novels that were more easily accessible to the general public and thus would sell better and would have a wider audience. I think there are numerous novelists that have done that, and that kind of thing is not going to pro-duce quite the great age of literature that we see among the moderns. But I think that it may be partly illusory that it isn't great, that there is not still great experimentation going on; I think of Beckett, for example, and perhaps Durrell.

WOOD: Are you saying that it's impossible to write fiction that could be both popular and of a high quality?

COWAN: No. I'm not saying that. But I'm saying that a great many novelists of the forties, for example, did react against the kind of experimentation that Woolf and Joyce and other writers of their generation had attempted to do and wrote more conventional novels of society, of the recognizable, easily identifiable social world and social surfaces.

GINDIN: I'd like to answer that in another way, too, which you may think is somewhat perverse, without for a moment derogating Woolf or Joyce or Lawrence, but recognizing how really great they are. I sometimes think that they wrote a kind of great fiction because they believed in greatness, that the whole idea—as Virginia Woolf herself said—was that "we are trembling on one of the great ages of English literature." There was a belief—in part individual and in part a part of their age—that dedication to art, intelligence, and great activity could somehow transform experience. It seems to me this is also a belief that has been considerably less visible among intellectuals since. And, in part—and it's only in part—the attempt to be great helps to create greatness. For example, when Mr. Unterecker was talking, one became aware that the last thing Henry Green or Beckett would ever say was, "I am going to be great and this is one of the great ages in literature."

Well, perhaps real greatness, if there is such a thing—and I wonder if there is such a thing—requires the belief in it. And I would also argue most of the time that there is a great deal of highly interesting fiction where the question of greatness in that way doesn't have to come out.

ROSSMAN: I've got something to add, too. It occurs to me that, since Mr. Gindin and Alan Friedman have both been perverse, we might extend Alan's kind of perversity, which was to transcend local boundaries and temporal periods, and notice that in South America a great many blockbuster novels are now being written. It seems to me hard to call the novel declining when Mario Vargas Llosa and Gabriel García Márquez and Julio Cortázar are all at the height of their prime. I might point out, too, that *Cien años de soledad* was often compared with Tolstoy when the reviews appeared.

COWAN: Or Nabokov or Beckett. I mean there are others that do fit the earlier mold.

DOBBS: I would like to ask Mr. Cowan, as the devil's advocate, if, in decrying accessibility, he and other modern critics might not be too favorably inclined toward obscurantism and experimentation in fiction.

COWAN: I don't think I am, because I think that Lawrence is quite accessible. This was the question that I chose to work with, and I was not particularly speaking of obscurantism so much as I was the willingness to break an old form. And this is partly what Lawrence was talking about in the passage I was quoting from *The Crown:* about having growth through destroying the old form, through breaking up the old pattern of a tight ego, being willing to break out and experiment—even to risk destruction in the process of it. And if I may use that as a metaphor for what people like Joyce and Woolf and Faulkner and others of their generation were doing: they were breaking the form of the well-made novel. I think there are those who are still doing this. I don't think they are the popular bestsellers quite frequently, although sometimes, as in the case of *Lolita,* for example, they are.

I'm not condemning accessibility, as such. Fielding, Richardson, people like that are accessible, and so is Faulkner in many of his works—so is Lawrence. I'm condemning rather an unwillingness to break an old reified pattern in order to assert a new sense of growth through the new form, because I think that is the only way it is asserted.

V E L Z : Would you regard the reified pattern, as Mr. Cowan calls it, as the Edwardian novel as described by Mr. Gindin, for example?

C O W A N : I think this is what Virginia Woolf described it as in her essay on modern fiction, the novel that she called the novel of the materialists. I am not at all sure that she was totally fair to Bennett, Galsworthy, and Wells in that statement. It seems to me that Bennett, for example in the *Old Wives' Tale* (if he's a materialist and describing a material reality), is describing a people whose consciousness derives from materialism; that is, what Marx referred to as the material basis of consciousness, the economic basis of consciousness. I think this is an aspect of Bennett that Mrs. Woolf doesn't mention in that essay.

Nevertheless, I think that she saw herself and the generation of novelists like her, like Joyce, for example, as breaking that old pattern. And she says that, whatever gifts we thank them for (and there are a great many), the sooner the English novel marches on, even if only into the desert, the better.

V E L Z : So the sort of novel that you are talking about in the forties and fifties would be, say, James Gould Cozzens...

C O W A N : I suppose.

V E L Z : ... in the mid-Victorian or Edwardian sense

of describing the society and the relationships within it.

UNTERECKER: C. P. Snow, now.

FLEISHMAN: Listening to the question and the answer, it occurs to me that, just as we have a need to adopt a different critical vocabulary from that of symbolism as opposed to realism, etc., we probably also need to have philosophical categories a little more subtle than materialism or even impressionism, which is a phrase used of Virginia Woolf that I think has been superseded. For a while I've been in love with the term *perspectivism,* which is, I think, what Mr. Unterecker was talking about very aptly. But I suppose I'll have to abandon that eventually, too. "Isms" in this realm, as they are in politics, are usually stultifying eventually.

COWAN: May I give an American example? Howells, in rebelling against what he called "romanticism," was rebelling against the kind of popular writers of his day who were presenting the reading public with a kind of watered-down version of Sir Walter Scott. And he admitted that romanticism in its day, in the day of Scott and other English Romantics, had served a very useful function in breaking an old pattern. But that by his day, say the 1870s, that kind of romanticism had become a form that needed to be broken also. We may still be in that system, too. I am not suggesting that novelists today need to ape Woolf and Joyce and Lawrence. They need to go on and be themselves and perhaps even break those patterns.

ROSSMAN: I would like to ask Joe Kruppa a question, if I can. I would like to know, Joe, if you feel like elaborating a bit on the innovation of Burroughs. Can you make the point that you were on the verge of making a while ago, or is now not the appropriate time?

MILLER: Yes. I didn't mean to make you stop talking. My answer was flippant.

KRUPPA: There are obvious similarities between Rabelais and Burroughs, both in thematic materials and scatological materials and also in terms of the encyclopedic nature of the books. But I think the similarities end there, and I think what's important about, for instance, Burroughs's breaking up of perspective is very, very different. And it's just that kind of rearrangement in the perspective, say, of dope pushers, that is new. It's too easy for us to say, ah, this is simply a convention from the past. And therefore maybe we should call this "Forms of Fiction," instead of "Modern British Fiction." I think the act of rearranging, when it's self-consciously arrived at as Burroughs did, is an important creative action.

MILLER: All I meant to say was to argue that the concept of modernism or novelty in any form of literature is a very problematic issue and that a great deal of care needs to be taken. We can agree that Burroughs is different from Rabelais, or from anybody else, and that the problem of defining that difference is much more of a challenge than at first it appears. Partly I think it's a limitation of our critical language; it's hard to find words. That's one of the reasons I'm a little suspicious of the perspectivism prospective: I'm not sure it does permit the identification of the differentials here.

UNTERECKER: What happens, though, if in a sense we are all consequences of the past? What do you do then with conspicuous differences in the past, say the eighteenth century and the sixteenth century, which really don't seem too much like each other?

GINDIN: To us?

UNTERECKER: To us. I don't think that the

eighteenth century felt that it was terribly like the sixteenth. When we look at differences in the past we see them as differences.

MILLER: Yes. There are similarities, too.

UNTERECKER: Oh, yes. But I think we are conscious of rather a difference in tone in, say, Alexander Pope and Shakespeare, or Marlowe.

GINDIN: But isn't this one of the ways that we appreciate them? I mean, isn't this a critically necessary act as we read to recognize that there is a great body of literature behind this and then to establish terms in our own minds by which we distinguish one from the other—simply, I think, as an act of the intelligence? In other words, if the intelligence is applying itself to a problem like that, it seems to be exercised better by asking, "What are the differences between this?" than by asking "What are the similarities?"

UNTERECKER: Although I would agree with Hillis, too, that when I take an individual line from Pope or an individual line from Shakespeare, I can say, "Gosh, they're remarkably similar to each other," and be overpowered with that, too.

MILLER: I'd like to not really answer that but shift a little bit and pick up something Alan said at the beginning, which seems the opposite of what I've been saying. I do have very strongly the feeling that the interpretation of narrative fiction right at this moment is a very exciting field and that there are breakthroughs taking place in this, whether we're applying ourselves to Fielding or Cervantes or Sterne or Beckett —that we could feel much more certain now than we did even ten years ago that we know what we're doing. It's also a kind of international and even interdisciplinary project in a way it wasn't before. This is going on in France. We are now covering the Russian formalists' approaches to these things. It's really a very exciting field for the study of literature at this moment. That would suggest something new, if not in the writers themselves, then in our ability to deal with them and talk about them.

UNTERECKER: And, in fact, literary critics, if they're going to be educated at all, certainly have to know, as I suggested, something about physics. They certainly have to know anthropology backward and forward.

COWAN: Is that something new, that they have to know something about Heisenberg?

UNTERECKER: Well, yes and no. But I think that, at least in parts of the nineteenth century, the feeling was that the literary critic at best needed to know something of history.

DOHERTY: I have a question that I would like to address particularly to Professor Miller because I think there is something new beyond just a mix: there's a quantum jump in discovering the architectonics of silence and emptiness. And here we are talking about the metaphysics of compositional strategy. Take one page from a passage in Beckett. Pim asks questions and gets answers. The answers aren't important. The page comes alive with the nervous moment, the intense moment when he asks the question and there is no answer. For that moment, we are drawn into the blankness of that space on the page. That is the nervous moment. And I don't know of anything before the twentieth century where the stylistic structure of emptiness and silence create a threat for the reader, and the meaning *is* the threat.

MILLER: You're pushing me very hard. I would

think there would be aspects again of Sterne that would be a kind of meticulous description of detail of physical objects, sort of drained of their significance.

COWAN: It occurs to me that all of the examples the audience are giving are from contemporary writers since the bomb.

MILLER: This, by the way, defines Sterne as something pretty extraordinary. He's one of those special kinds of writers who explode one's desire to put things in period compartments; in a way it's cheating a little to always be able to bring Sterne out as an answer to a question.

FRIEDMAN: It's nice that he's there.

MILLER: He existed, though.

MEMBER OF THE AUDIENCE: And then Robbe-Grillet: his language is so dry, stiff, antipoetic, in a way; he approaches people and objects in a very dry way.

MILLER: So is the end of *The Sentimental Journey* when Yorick reaches his hand out. It's described in somewhat the same way. I don't say that Robbe-Grillet is the same as Sterne but that again you have a case where there's a permutation of devices used to tell a story that have already been used. That's the point.

GINDIN: I would throw out another point on Robbe-Grillet and say that, methodologically, in the kind of filtering of every detail through a character, through a construct, there are times when some of Dickens's scenes and characters seem to me Robbe-Grilletish. Although, if you say "dryness," obviously that wouldn't fit Dickens. But part of the method, it seems to me, is Dickensian.

UNTERECKER: Yes, but you don't have the total impact of a Robbe-Grillet novel resembling the total impact of any novel that you can come up with; I honestly don't think you can. Sterne's tone is not Robbe-Grillet's tone.

MEMBER OF THE AUDIENCE: It's a great change in literary conception that makes Robbe-Grillet, Robbe-Grillet and Dickens, Dickens.

FLEISHMAN: I would like you gentlemen to consider something of Jane Austen's that might qualify as having the same dryness, coldness, meticulousness: the working out of a set of propositions with ironic discoveries of the implications of convention and of form, *Northanger Abbey.*

MILLER: I still think there is a danger that we might think of ourselves as living in a kind of totally extreme world that's radically different from the experience that human beings ever had before. I have the feeling that it may not be quite so bad as that or that it has always been as bad as that, and that great writers of the past, like Ben Jonson, for example, had the same insights into the power of language that even James Joyce has had. I would pick up one thing that's been said, though, that I think is very important and might provide an alternative to the emphasis we've been putting on the sort of optical metaphor or model for thinking about these writers; an alternative way in which you might get at the modernity of modern writing is to say that people like Joyce and post-Joyceans are perhaps more overtly aware that literature is made of language. And they incorporate into their texts an alternative model to the perspectivist one, namely, the one that says the human situation is not that of somebody looking at something, not the epistemological or optical situation, but the situation of a reader of a text. A book like *Finnegans Wake* is ostentatiously made out of language. And this again is part of the tradition, as Avrom Fleishman brilliantly showed, that literature has always involved parody, the use of earlier works of literature. There does seem to be a new kind of intensification of that awareness in the twentieth century in a writer like John Barth, for example.

V E L Z : That would imply, wouldn't it, that there is a discontinuity between the nineteenth and twentieth centuries?

M I L L E R : Well, I've been trying to argue that, but—

V E L Z : But, the point is that nobody is more allusive than Joyce, surely, and yet your inclination was to reach back into the period in which you've done most of your work and find the same thing going on in the middle of the nineteenth century.

M I L L E R : Well, my inclination was to say that a great writer like Joyce picks up part of the tradition and, so to speak, brings it out into the open and exploits it to the very limit. In the same way, you could say that one way to define *Remembrance of Things Past* is to say that Proust takes the conventions of nineteenth-century realist fiction and pushes them to a point where they explode and go beyond themselves. But those are the conventions that he was working within, and Joyce does the same thing. There is nothing in *Ulysses* that isn't in some way prepared for by earlier fiction. And yet, there is nothing like *Ulysses* anywhere in Victorian fiction.

F L E I S H M A N : Is the appropriate use of this heightened consciousness of language, the appropriate use of that concept, simply to say that modern fiction suggests that we are all experiencing the world of the text, or is it rather that we are all in the condition of the writer, trying to make sense of our experiences and, as it were, reduplicating the novelist's effort to write a novel? The novelist is, as it were, our hero, going out ahead of us to do what we are all doing, willy-nilly, in daily life.

UNTERECKER: I was trying to suggest very much that point in what I've been saying. In a way, what we do is to participate in a much more subconscious way than we usually do in the process of looking at reality in a lot of the fiction that's being written in our time. And the novelist forces us to be aware of that process.

Now, it's true that there are lots of novels again that have done this in the past; *Tristram Shandy* is the conspicuous example, it seems to me. But I think it's more characteristic of the twentieth century. In a sense, we really do have to be in on the novelist's or the poet's sense of Beckett's "How it is." And his sense of "How it is-ness" is what involves us. We become less interested in the characters and more interested in the ways of seeing. I think that, for instance, when you talk of Beckett's having entered a world in which nothingness becomes important, it really is saying that this is a way of seeing that is characteristic of some people in the twentieth century and that it is an important way of seeing. Or, when you say that we become aware of the silences between the words, you're saying again that we've become aware of the fact that words aren't the only methods by which we communicate. And we've become very conscious of this, it seems to me, not just in terms of a sense of the limits of language but also increasingly in the sciences—particularly the biological sciences—of a sense that there are all kinds of languages. There are languages, not just of little things like gesture and bodily languages, but there are obvious techniques of communication: heat-transfer languages, if you have to use a word like that.

I think we have the sense again of a world that is not separated from man and a sense that man sees analogous things going on in the world that resemble his methods of perception but that are different. One of the things the novelist forces us to do is to participate with him in the discovery of that kind of world. I think that a reader who comes across Sartre's extraordinary novel *Nausea* for the first time and sees that monster tree growing there represented as pure being, while the central character leans on a bench beside it and feels himself in the tree in a process of mere being, has an immense jolt come over him. It's an altogether different way of apprehending things than nineteenth-century fiction apprehended.

FLEISHMAN: But the necessary consequences of that perception is to go out and write a novel as Roquentin does at the end of *La Nausée.*

UNTERECKER: Exactly. It throws us into the novelist's role by opening up experience to us and demanding that we, in a sense, participate in the writing of the novel; I was trying to suggest that the work of art coming out and grabbing us and saying, you're part of me, is again, I think, peculiar in some ways to the twentieth century, though not entirely. Whitman, after all, was saying, who knows but that I'm looking forward to you looking back on me in a hundred years after I'm dead.

DOHERTY: When I raised the issue of silences and empty spaces in the Beckett passage, I was thinking of his trying to create total existence there, what the physicists identify as black holes: just cave-ins into nonbeing or "being" so dense it can't be directly perceived. And so it's not a question of other means of communication in our language, but of gaps in existence across which there is nothing, and the artist contrives to maneuver his reader into these untenable spaces.

R O S S M A N : Sterne also includes a black page.

G I N D I N : I want to throw out another name, simply because in the last three or four days we haven't mentioned him. But one of the most interesting novelists who, for me at any rate, unless I don't understand him, is full of spaces and black spots and questions like that is Meredith. And I always wonder how one talks about him.

M I L L S : A black hole is a body of matter so dense that the intensity of its gravitational field prevents the escape of any radiation, and I wonder if you gentlemen are talking about black spots or black holes? I have felt all along that there has been an unarticulated proposition spiraling around and around. This proposition might be expressed as the idea that the modern critic and the modern novelist are both grappling with the possibility that there are kinds of order our brains are not capable of grasping—an idea that has emerged dramatically in this century, especially from science. Is that what you're talking about?

M I L L E R : Like Beckett's interrogator, you should say.

U N T E R E C K E R : I think it's a sense that many novelists have, but I don't know if it's—

M I L L S : In other words, are you talking about a black spot—a void—or a black hole—a concentration or density beyond our comprehension? I was very much struck last night by Mr. Miller's marvelous paper. I enjoyed it immensely; can I criticize it a little bit?

M I L L E R : Cummings said that; feel free.

M I L L S : The one thing that I really expected J. Hillis Miller to say, he didn't say. That is, he talked so interestingly about Hardy's projection of sequence, and he wound up with a picture, a model, that seems essentially to conform to our contemporary drive for new and unfamiliar concepts of order. But you left this model hanging, it seems to me, because it was Hardy who did this. The poor guy worked like a dog making all these patterns that cancel each other out. Now, I wish you would say something about a relationship I know you've thought about. Hardy didn't really express a sense of his own drive in creating his patterns, but this is something you can express. Am I making sense?

MILLER: Yes, although I guess silence is still the proper answer to that. I haven't any words of wisdom, neither a yes nor a no like the character in Beckett— except to say that one of the problems there with the notion of an order that exceeds our power to grasp it is that there is no way of telling whether you're dealing with a black spot, where there isn't anything, or a black hole, where there is an excessive plentitude, I should think.

MILLS: The thing is, as I keep insisting in my own mind, Hardy was a conscious thinker; the novel wasn't just a form: it was the living spirit of Hardy. A scholar we both admire, Mr. Poulet, has dealt so interestingly with that idea. Could you talk about it from that point of view?

MILLER: I could, but I don't think I will, partly because at the moment, in the work I'm doing, I'm inclined to think that the concept of consciousness may be one of those misleading invitations to solve the problem of a difficult literary text like *Tess of the D'Urbervilles,* or any of the others we've been talking about, by hypothesizing an explanation of it in terms of a fixed origin, such as, in this case, the consciousness of the author. And I'm not sure that, in the case of *Tess of the D'Urbervilles,* that's really going to help, if only because all we really know about the consciousness of Hardy, all that really matters, is the text of *Tess of the D'Urbervilles* and the other things that Hardy wrote.

In other words, the consciousness that we're dealing with is one that is entirely embodied in language. This is an insight that Georges Poulet also has, by the way, in the way in which his own criticism, say in the wonderful sequence of Proust essays, has to go beyond itself and put in question its own apparent commitment to the notion of consciousness as a sort of priority that will allow you to explain all the complexity of a given work.

MILLS: Thank you.

FRIEDMAN : I think no ultimate summation at this point is possible. It may not be necessary either. I would only say, with all of you, thank you very much.

Notes on Contributors

James Cowan, founder and editor of the *D. H. Lawrence Review,* is professor of English at the University of Arkansas. His publications include numerous articles on Lawrence; articles on Pound, William Carlos Williams, Hart Crane, Faulkner, and Jonathan Edwards; and a recent book, *D. H. Lawrence's American Journey.* Among works in progress are an *Annotated Bibliography of Lawrence,* a concordance to Lawrence's poetry, a collection of previously unpublished Lawrence materials, and a book on intellectual backgrounds to modern literature. "D. H. Lawrence's Dualism" represents an important part of this last work.

Avrom Fleishman is professor of English at Johns Hopkins University and editor and contributor to *ELH: A Journal of English Literary History.* His studies of the British novel have appeared in such other journals as *Contemporary Literature, Criticism, English Literature in Transition, Nineteenth-Century Fiction,* and *Studies in English Literature.* His books have treated *Mansfield Park,* Conrad's politics, and the English historical novel. "Virginia Woolf: Tradition and Modernity" is part of a recently completed book on Woolf's fiction. His various awards include a Guggenheim fellowship and an American Council of Learned Societies grant-in-aid; he has been voted an outstanding teacher by Johns Hopkins students.

Alan Warren Friedman has taught British and American literature at the University of Texas at Austin since 1964. He has published a book on Lawrence Durrell and essays on such writers as Philip Roth, Bernard Malamud, Henry Miller, Joyce Cary, Joseph Conrad, and Christopher Marlowe. Forthcoming work includes a study of narrative in twentieth-century fiction, *Multivalence: The Moral Quality of Form in the Modern Novel*. He has spent a year at the University of Edinburgh and one at the University of Bristol, the latter as a National Endowment for the Humanities Fellow. He is director of Plan II, the multidisciplinary honors program at the University of Texas at Austin.

James Gindin is professor of English at the University of Michigan. He has published articles on such writers as Fitzgerald, Mailer and Updike, Lawrence, Golding, Murdoch, and Sillitoe in journals that include the *Centennial Review, Contemporary Literature, Modern Fiction Studies, Modern Language Quarterly, Texas Quarterly,* and *Texas Studies.* He has also edited a critical edition of Hardy's *Return of the Native* and written two wide-ranging studies, *Postwar British Fiction* and the recent *Harvest of a Quiet Eye: The Novel of Compassion*. Professional activities include numerous commissioned book reviews; radio, television, and university lectures; a Fulbright lectureship at the University of Sheffield; a National Endowment for the Humanities fellowship; and a year as checker in the editorial department of the *New Yorker*.

After nineteen years at Johns Hopkins University
(including three as department chairman), J. Hillis
Miller is now professor of English at Yale University.
His major publications include books on Dickens and
Hardy, two on nineteenth-century writers, and *Poets of
Reality: Six Twentieth-Century Writers;* he has edited
collections of essays on William Carlos Williams and
Wallace Stevens, as well as *Modern Language Notes,
ELH: A Journal of English Literary History,* and *College English,* and has written numerous articles on
subjects ranging from *Huckleberry Finn* to the Geneva
School of Criticism. His many awards include an American Philosophical Society grant, two Guggenheim
fellowships, and a Danforth Foundation Harbison
teaching award.

A former Peace Corps volunteer and Fulbright lec-
turer at National University of Mexico, Charles Rossman is associate professor of English at the University
of Texas at Austin. A member of the editorial boards
of *Texas Studies in Literature and Language* and the
D. H. Lawrence Review, he has contributed three essays
on Lawrence to the latter. Pending publication is a
long essay, "D. H. Lawrence and Women," in a volume
of new Lawrence materials and essays; he is a con-
tributing editor to the forthcoming *Annotated Bibliography of D. H. Lawrence.* A second study of Joyce's
Portrait is forthcoming in the *James Joyce Quarterly.*

After many years as professor of English at Columbia University, John Unterecker now teaches at the
University of Hawaii. His extensive publications include
three books written or edited on Yeats, a monograph
on Lawrence Durrell, a children's book, dozens of

poems, articles, and reviews in such journals as *American Scholar, Evergreen Review,* the *Nation, New York Times Book Review, Poetry, Sewanee Review,* and *Yale Review.* His *Voyager: A Life of Hart Crane* received the Van Amringe best-book-of-the-year award and was nominated for a National Book Award. He has received American Council of Learned Societies and American Philosophical Society grants, summer fellowships to Yaddo for creative work in poetry, and a Guggenheim fellowship; he has done considerable work in radio, television, and off-Broadway theater. Work now in progress includes two books of poems, a novel, and a book on the plays of W. B. Yeats. He was a visiting professor at the University of Texas at Austin in spring 1974.

Index

242 | Index